# The Practical Guide to the Control of Feral Cats

Stephen M. Vantassel

Wildlife Control Consultant, LLC
Lincoln, Nebraska
2013

ISBN 978-0-9668582-7-3

Design and composition, using Segoe UI types, by Paul Royster.

# Contents

# Introduction

According to the American Pet Products Association (APPA), the domestic house cat (*Felis catus*) is the most popular pet in the U.S. by total numbered owned (86.4 million). Dogs, which came in second at 76.2 million, are owned by more households (46.3 million versus 38.9 million for cats). No matter how you calculate, we have a lot of cats in the U.S. But these numbers don't tell the whole story. For there are an estimated 60 million more that are feral or unowned cats, roaming in the U.S. But whether wild or not, cats often are allowed by custom, regulation, and ordinance, the privilege to roam free. Unlike wildlife, which landowners can often remove from their property, cats are essentially a protected predator. The feral cat lobby, or as I like to call them the free-range cat lobby, are a highly organized and highly vocal group that religiously support the notion that cats should be allowed to roam free no matter what.

This book is dedicated to helping landowners suffering under the paw of these free-range cats. I have written this book to empower them regarding ways to manage the menace of free-range cats. This book will provide effective methods to control free-range cats. The book contains information gleaned from my own work, the experience of others, and research related to cats and their control. I have endeavored to acknowledge sources in the references list at the end of each chapter. It isn't the complete guide to cat control because I don't cover every potential control method. But the information provided here covers the fundamentals.

Readers may think that in order to write such a book, I must hate cats. Such is not the case. I became a cat lover around 1998 when my wife picked up a rescue from the local pound. The policy of the pound was to euthanize adult cats after holding them for only 3 days. The cat we ultimately adopted was on his second day. I am not criticizing the pound. Most people don't want adult cats so the pound's policy was extremely understandable and appropriate. When my wife brought this cat home, I can only say, that he purred his way into my heart. But we didn't let him roam free. He was an indoor cat. Contrary to popular mythology, cats don't die when they're kept indoors. Instead they are protected from injuries that they can sustain from being outdoors as well as prevented from inflicting injuries on our native wildlife. Furthermore an indoor cat is less likely to spread disease to others, particularly, its owners. More information about all of these elements will follow in this book. But let the reader understand and banish any notion that the author hates cats. Only those deliberately seeking to mislead others would suggest otherwise.

In the development of this book, I have tried to keep in mind 2 audiences, landowners and professional vertebrate control technicians. I don't always keep them separate. Readers should determine for themselves whether a certain point concerns them. Finally, the book is intended to be read as a unit. Avoid the tendency to read just the chapters you think are important as you may miss an essential warning or fact.

## Resources

Industry Trends and Statistics. 2012. Pet Ownership in the U.S. American Pet Products Association. http://americanpetproducts.org/press_industrytrends.asp visited June 3, 2012.

Hildreth, A., S. Vantassel, and S. Hygnstrom. 2010. *Feral Cats and Their Management*. EC1781. University of Nebraska-Lincoln.

# Acknowledgments

I would like to thank the reviewers who have edited this book. Their willingness to provide me the benefit of their expertise and photos has improved the quality of this book. They have been kept anonymous for their protection. I am grateful to all of them for their invaluable insight.

# About the Author

**Stephen M. Vantassel** has been involved in wildlife damage management since 1984. His articles have appeared in *Journal of Wildlife Management, The Wildlife Professional, Wildlife Control Technology, Pest Control Technology, Fur, Fish, and Game,* and others. He is the former owner of Wildlife Removal Service, Inc., (sold in 1998), and has held wildlife control licenses in 3 states.

His accomplishments include, Educator of the Year award from the National Wildlife Control Operators Association (2008 and 2012), Certified Wildlife Control Professional (2001), Academy Certified Professional (2007), and Master NWCOA Instructor (2012). He has written several books, including Dominion over Wildlife? An Environmental-Theology of Human-Wildlife Relations (2009) and The National Wildlife Control Training Program (2012).

He is the Program Coordinator for wildlife damage management at the University of Nebraska-Lincoln, where he educates the public about wildlife damage management through the Internet Center for Wildlife Damage Management, http://icwdm.org

Stephen presently owns Wildlife Control Consultant, LLC, a firm that helps clients with wildlife conflicts through research, writing, and training. He is available for speaking, training, and consultation. He can be contacted through his website, http://wildlifecontrolconsultant.com

Stephen's comments are his own and do NOT reflect the views of the University of Nebraska–Lincoln.

# Disclaimer

I could not and will not take the time to determine or discuss the laws concerning the control of cats in your state or locale. You, the reader, are responsible for ascertaining the laws and regulations regarding the management of cats in your area. Ignorance of the law is no excuse. Additionally, even if you follow the law, don't assume you are immune from prosecution. Additionally, you must consider how you might be vilified by the free-range cat lobby when it learns of your activity.

While sympathetic to the plight of landowners and wildlife being harmed by the ecological menace known as free-range cats, I do not endorse nor do I recommend breaking the law, no matter how stupid or anti-environmental it might be. Unfortunately, too many Americans selectively exempt themselves from the rules rather than work to change them. I encourage everyone to help their politicians find the moral backbone necessary to stand up for the environment and assert the right of landowners and environmentalists to protect their property and native species from the menace of free-range cats. Our wildlife populations, particularly our songbirds, are in desperate need of our support.

Control of cats, as with all vertebrate species, involves risk to those performing the control. These risks include, but are not limited to, physical injury (up to and including debilitating injuries that may lead to death), diseases (up to and including infections that can lead to severe morbidity and even death). Readers perform vertebrate control at their own risk. The author has endeavored to provide information about the risks and how to mitigate and reduce those risks. Nevertheless, it is impossible to cover all the risks those engaged in the control of cats may face.

It is always better to hire a qualified professional rather than put yourself at risk. Vertebrate control, including the control of cats, is not rocket science. However, dealing with animals always involves risk as their behavior is never completely predictable. Additionally, it is easy to cut corners and side-step safety practices because you don't want to be bothered with putting on gloves etc. Carelessness begins with the attitude that says, "I don't need to do xyz because this task is too simple."

The mentioning of particular products and brand names does not necessarily constitute an endorsement of a product nor does the lack of mention of a product necessarily imply criticism. Readers are encouraged to carefully investigate products before purchase.

# Chapter 1. **The Challenge**

As mentioned in the introduction, house cats (*Felis catus*) are the most popular pet in the U.S. But it's not the number of cats that is the problem, it is what owners and officials have allowed cats to do.

House cats pose 3 significant problems, each of which are under appreciated by the public to varying degrees. The first, and least notable, problem is the nuisance value of cats. Landowners, particularly gardeners, frequently complain about cats using their land for litter boxes. For others, the territorial spraying by male cats and the accompanying odor is problematic. The second problem is the way cats can vector diseases to human populations. Cats, in this regard, are no better or worse than many other species. The difference is that humans are taught to avoid direct contact with wildlife. The same can't be said of cats. Most cat owners don't even realize how letting their cat out at night and then in during the day is the moral equivalent of playing disease roulette with their family. Chapter 3 will discuss this issue in more detail. The final problem is the most well-known. It concerns the impact cats have on native populations of wildlife. Put simply, cats are protected invasive predators. The evidence is so overwhelming that I won't go into it. Of course, you can go to the feral cat lobby groups and get "another opinion."

Since the behavior and status of cats depends on the situation, I will use the following definitions to keep things straight in this chapter. House cats will refer to cats kept indoors or restricted by means of a physical barrier to the landowner's property. Free-range cats will refer to cats whose owners allow the cats to leave the property and trespass on the property of others. Feral cats are those lacking owners.

**The Legal Gray Areas**

Presently, most states categorize cats as domestic animals (as opposed to wildlife). This fact has 3 implications. First, cats are considered private property. If you catch a cat and euthanize it, be aware that the burden of proof is on you to show the cat wasn't owned. You may find that the cat is not owned if it did something wrong (like biting someone) but quickly becomes "owned" if you did something wrong or perceived wrong. Some locales state that if the cats are fed for period of time, then the feeders become the de facto owners. Second, cats as domestic animals are protected by more restrictive anti-cruelty laws. While wildlife are also protected by cruelty laws, they are significantly less restrictive. For example, you can shoot a deer but you probably can't or at least shouldn't shoot your dog. Third, in some areas the fact that cats are domestic animals means you are not allowed to kill cats at all. While I disagree with this restriction (as I will explain below), it at least makes it clear what you or your company can or cannot do in regards to controlling cats.

But for many states, the legal status of cats remains fuzzy because states won't discuss the status of feral cats (i.e. cats that lack owners). Don't think that you are free from problems by getting client assurances that the cats you are trapping are feral. Just because a cat is feral doesn't mean someone doesn't consider himself or herself to be an owner. It is an interesting Catch-22. If the feral cat bites someone, many of these so called owners disavow ownership. They will say that they just fed the cat. If you trap the same cat they will claim you are stealing their property. Add to this conundrum the problem of free-range cats. Feral cats are different than free-range cats. Free-range cats are owned but their owners believe the cat has a right to roam wherever it wants. In fact, city ordinances may even support such a notion.

Unfortunately, many governments (whether state or municipal) often don't provide any legal protection to property owners suffering damage from cats. If the cats are trapped, then you may run afoul of laws related to domestic animals or be cited for working beyond the scope of your license or other legal authority.

The fourth problem is that even if you are allowed to control "feral cats" or that feral cats have no legal protections, you may still encounter problems from public opinion that opposes lethal control of cats. Control of cats is a legal and public relations labyrinth where one misstep can drop you into nightmare with significant legal and financial impacts.

Bottom line, before starting any cat control, check with your state and local governments. If it is permissible or not forbidden (which is not the same thing legally speaking, just ask a lawyer), proceed with extreme caution if you decide you want to engage in cat control services. Second, if you decide to control cats have a plan for handling them, ask if you can bring the cats to a shelter. While many shelters won't accept the cats ahead of time, or if they do, they may only

hold them a few days, obtaining their help spreads the responsibility and often gives time for owners to reclaim their cats. You could
try to announce to the neighborhood that you are controlling cats.
But if you do, don't be surprised at the backlash. Many cat owners (a
term I use to include members of the feral cat feeders) believe that
the U.S. Constitution and God Himself support a cat's right to roam
free. They will refuse to keep their cats indoors during the few days
you will be trapping. Another option is to obtain an order from the
local Health Department to remove the stray cats. Health depart-
ments have wide powers that could be used in your defense should
a legal problem ever arise. A final option is to sell or rent a trap to
property owners so they can trap the cats themselves. Just be sure
that if you decide to do cat control as a business or rent out traps to
others, that you have appropriate liability protection in place. Whatever decision you make, be discreet and totally professional as in
"you would be proud if your actions were videotaped and the video
went viral."

## Other Legal Risks

Even when running a legal operation, legal risks remain. Whenever
fee-based services are provided, one enters into contractual relations with a client. Contracts imply responsibility and with responsibility comes the legal (and moral) obligation to perform work according to accepted standards. Of course, this begs the question,
"What is the accepted standard for the control of house cats?"
While there may be no codified standard for operating a cat control company, there are several principles that should be followed.

First, as noted above, FOLLOW THE LAW. Don't cut corners. But
following the law may not be enough. So to be safer, follow the second principle, namely, use the most effective, humane, responsible
techniques to control this cat problem, for example, it may be legal
to use traditional footholds to capture cats in your state. But if you
can still accomplish the job with padded-jaw footholds, then this
would be a better choice, because you have made efforts to reduce
the risk of stress and injury to the cats. Likewise, conibear-style traps
may be legal in your state. Have you made sure that the conibear-
style traps close tightly and have strong springs to help ensure the
likelihood of rapid death? Or is it wiser to capture as many cats as
you can with cages before turning to conibear-style traps or other
control techniques?

Third, how often are you checking traps? Will trapped animals have water and shelter available to them while they wait for you to come? Consult with animal control officers in your municipality and ask what their standard of practice is for controlling cats. If you abide by their standard of care, it is likely that you will have reduced the chances of being charged with animal cruelty (remember that the officers may have more privileges than you will have).

Remember, these standards are fluid in that what was acceptable 10 years ago may not be acceptable today. Just like surgery, practices change and hopefully improve. Dr. Schmidt of Utah State University has a good advice when he says, "Don't do anything that you wouldn't mind being on the front page of the newspaper tomorrow." If you assume you are always being watched, you will avoid doing something that can be perceived as cruel unless the person is an animal rights activist.

Other legal risks face you or your company. If a mature woman can sue McDonalds over a spilled cup of hot coffee and win, how much more vulnerable are you when controlling cats? While it is fun to beat up on lawyers, the fact is many lawsuits frequently occur because of shoddy workmanship. The key to preventing lawsuits is always to maintain the highest ethical standards both in your practices and in the quality of your workmanship.

To reduce your liability, consider the following strategies. Modify these suggestions as necessary if you are controlling cats on your own land.

First, utilize legal protections for businesses. Incorporate or create a limited liability corporation for your business. Consult your attorney and/an accountant on which type best meets your needs.

Second, obtain liability insurance. Consult with your insurance agency to ensure you have the right protection. Don't forget your vehicle needs to be included too.

Third, do quality work. This means you must not only do a quality job (no cutting corners), but you must document your activities as well. As we say in the medical field, "If it isn't written down, it didn't happen."

Fourth, report your findings to your client. Failure to inform your client of potential risks (e.g. fecal deposits) may lead to legal liability on your part. Complete and detailed documentation also protects you.

Remember these key points for documentation:

- Take photos of key areas on the property before and during your inspection. If you are performing control or mitigation, be sure to take photos following your activities.

- Take detailed notes.
- Carry government-created fact sheets on rabies, raccoon roundworm, and others that can be left with clients.
- Direct clients to other sources of information by noting them on your paperwork.
- Have clients sign your paperwork to acknowledge receipt.

If you think that I have overstated or hyped the concerns you should have before beginning to control cats, read Chapter 12 of Jim Sterba's book, *Nature Wars*.

## Resources

Ash, S. J. and C. E. Adams. 2003. Public Preferences for Free-Ranging Domestic Cat (*Felis catus*) Management Options. *Wildlife Society Bulletin* 31:2(Summer):334-339.

Sterba, J. 2012. *Nature Wars: The Incredible Story of How Wildlife Comebacks Turned Backyards in Battlegrounds.* NY, NY: Crown Publishers.

Chapter 2. **The Biology of the House Cat**

### Description

Cats (*Felis catus*) are small to medium sized predators (Fig. 1). They are small in stature, weighing from 3 to 8 pounds (1.4 to 3.6 kg; though 1 source said that most breeds weigh between 2.5 to 7.0 kg), standing 8 to 12 inches (20 to 30.5 cm) high at the shoulder, and are 14 to 24 inches (35.5 to 61 cm) long. The tail adds another 8 to 12 inches (20 to 30.5 cm) to their length. Males are larger than females, with females about 80% of the weight of males. Colors range from black to white to orange, and any combination in between. Cats have 4 types of fur, guard hairs, awn hairs, awned down-hairs, and down-hairs which are located on different parts of their body.

Cats typically have 4 toes and a heel pad (Fig. 2). Unfortunately, some cats have more than 4 toes and others may have less than 4. Claws are retractable in adults and typically will not be seen in tracks. Foot order in walking is front foot and back foot on the same side then the other front and back feet move on the other side. This is unusual in that most 4-legged species walk in alternating fashion, front leg on one side, then the rear leg on the other side, then back to the other side.

**Fig. 1.** *House cat. No collar, no tags, no restrictions on movement.*

**Life History**

Cats reach sexual maturity quickly (within 5 to 6 months of age). Males are promiscuous and are able to impregnate multiple females. After mating, females cry out, and turn against their paramour. Once separated, cats will wash themselves. Pregnant females give birth to 1 to 6 kittens in 65 days. Females in lower latitudes have more litters than those in higher latitudes but the average is 1.6 times per year. To put into context, even where cats have a high death rate, their reproductive capacity is high enough to maintain the population. Expect ½ of the females to be pregnant during the spring. That figure can drop to 4% between October and January.

Females, particularly those living with other females, may move young before week 6. Females don't build nests but will exploit available shelters. Shelters that protect the cats from wind and rain are preferred. Kittens need about 30 days to achieve sufficient motor and sensory abilities comparable to a young child. Nursing of young also diminishes around day 30. Nursing females expend a lot of energy nursing young and can lose 5.7g per day on average and can be quite nutritionally stressed beginning on week 6 when young begin to move away from the mother.

Young are vulnerable to a number of threats including chilling, dehydration, and predation. High mortality is not unheard of. One study found that ¾ of all kittens died or disappeared within 6

**Fig. 2.** *Cat track.*

months of birth. One source said females only raise 1.5 young per year to full maturity. Trauma was the primary cause of death, with dog attacks and motor vehicle collisions being the most common. Male cats will kill young. Females must find a nesting location to protect them from those threats. Young that die may be consumed by their mothers. It is believed that feral cats have an average life span of about 5 years.

Cats shed their fur throughout the year but it is most intense spring though early fall when temperatures change the most.

## Capabilities

Cats have a variety of abilities that enable them to be effective predators.

Their ears can turn just over 180° allowing them to listen to noises without having to turn their head. They can hear at a frequency of 30 to 50,000 cycles/second which is about 25,000 cycles higher than the highest notes on a violin or the limits of human hearing. Cats have the ability to distinguish sounds at 60 feet which are only 18 inches apart. Though cats can walk quietly, it is not so quiet that cats can't hear other cats approaching.

Cats can leap 71 inches with some reports up to 10 feet. During the jump they can twist and turn their body to position themselves better in the capture of prey. They can right themselves within a distance of their own height to ensure they land on their feet. Cats can also survive high falls of 12 ft or more. One researcher believed that cats reach terminal velocity of 40 mph within 60 feet.

Cats are also rather good climbers of trees and even ladders. I have personally witnessed a cat on the roof of a building (Fig. 3a). It had climbed up the tree on the opposite end (Fig. 3b). Of course, cats are better at climbing up than climbing down.

Cats have good vision, particularly in low light conditions. They have a reflective membrane that allows their eyes to reflect available light to the brain. It's that membrane that gives the cat's eyes that glow when a light is shined at them. Cats have a wide field of vision up to 280 degrees. Eighty degrees is monocular vision (each side) and 180 degrees is binocular. Their binocular vision enables them to judge distances well. They sway their heads back and forth to help them judge distance. Cats can't see well in the middle of their binocular vision. They are most attuned to movement picked up in their peripheral vision. Cats are not color blind but their ability to distinguish colors is poor. Research shows they can distinguish red from blue, gray,

**Fig. 3a.** *House cat stranded on roof of second floor.*

**Fig. 3b.** *The tree the cat used to get there.*

green, green from blue, and gray, and yellow from blue and gray. Research is trying to determine if they can distinguish red from yellow.

Cats have a good sense of smell. Their nose has 67,000,000 receptors compared with 20,000,000 for us. They use this sense to identify pheromones left by other cats.

Cat skin is remarkably sensitive to touch but not temperature change. Cats won't be disturbed until temperature reaches 124°F. Cat whiskers are either black or white and are used to help it sense its environment by helping them determine whether they can fit into an opening. They occur in 4 rows and extend beyond the width of the head.

Cat sensitivity to taste is greatest when temperature is 86°F. Cat taste ability in progressive order of strength is sweet, salt, bitter, then sour. Understanding that their sensitivity to sweetness is weak will be important when using baits. Cats have strong digestive juices capable of softening bones. These digestive juices are important because their bite-force is actually below average for their body mass when compared to other carnivores with a bite force quotient of 84.4 (100 is considered average). Using Newtons for a scale, cats have a bite force at the canine tips of 73.3 and at the carnassial eocone (the edge where upper and lower teeth meet resulting in shearing action) of 118.1.

## Behavior

Cats can be active any time of day though dusk to dawn is preferred. Like humans that are either right- or left-handed, most cats also prefer one front paw over the other. One study found that 38% of cats were left-handed, 20% were right-handed and 42% were ambidextrous.

Cats sleep lightly and they can be easily awakened with sound or vibration. The term "cat nap" underscores the light resting of a cat that is not fully asleep as denoted by its ears twitching to get a better grasp of unfamiliar sounds.

## Communication

Cats employ a variety of forms of communication. The role and importance of these forms of communication are not equally understood.

**Odor.** Urine from cats is quite pungent with male urine significantly more odorous than females due to the higher concentration of sulfurous compounds. Males are more likely to spray vertical surfaces than females. Cats do investigate the urine markings of others with males showing especial interest.

**Feces.** Cats typically bury feces near their home ranges but will leave them exposed elsewhere. These locations are calling areas and not defended.

**Scratching.** Scratching not only sharpens claws and helps the cat stretch, but it also deposits odors from the glands in the feet.

**Skin glands.** Cats have several glands in their skin. Head and chin rubbing are 2 sites where cats deposit glandular material on objects and each other.

## Sound Communication

Purrs and meows are the most common vocalizations. Other sounds can be heard including screech for pain and hisses for aggression. Caterwauling occurs primarily during mating season but can be heard at other times.

## Visual Communication

Cats can exhibit a variety of postures to signal emotions. Tail between legs signals fear and submission. Arched back with tail erect and mouth open shows aggression or fear. Tail motions can express anger (whipping back and forth) to disgust (the single flip) as it walks away. Ears and facial expressions are also important indicators of emotion. Since the cat's mouth is of great concern (you don't want to be bitten), I will focus on 4 facial expressions (Figs. 4a–d).

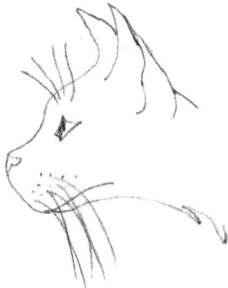

**Fig. 4a.** *Ears forward — Interest*     **Fig. 4b.** *Ears flat — Frightened*

**Fig. 4c.** *Ears back and erect — Puzzled*     **Fig. 4d.** *Mouth open and ears back — Furious*

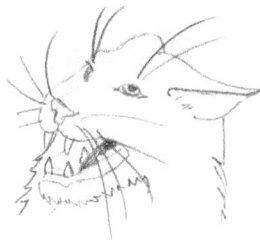

## Hunting

Cats can cover a large area or a small one, depending on their resource needs. A review of the various studies stated that the home range of cats varied 1000% (No that isn't a typo). The statistic held true for male and female cats, but males tend to roam over larger areas. How far cats roam or don't ultimately depends on the situation in your area. In urban areas, cats tend to remain within 5 hectares. In agricultural areas, cats can range out to 200 hectares. It is not unheard of to have cats hunting up to 2 miles from their den. Cats utilize hearing as their primary means of identifying the presence of prey. Once a cat's attention is alerted by auditory clues, its vision comes into play. Cats employ both waiting and stalking hunting behaviors. A cat tends to stalk and creep toward prey, freezing as necessary until it is close enough to pounce.

Cats can hunt during the day or at night and are generally solitary hunters. One study found that cats killed 50% of prey during daylight, 20% at dusk/dawn, and 30% at night. Birds tended to be caught during the morning, reptiles in the afternoon, frogs and mammals at night. The largest animal cats tend to kill is the Norway rat (which weigh up to a pound), but tree squirrels and rabbits are also taken. Cats seem to be drawn to newly mowed fields, perhaps because the cutting makes prey more vulnerable. Hunting and killing is NOT stopped by feeding. Cats are instinctual hunters/killers and well-fed cats continue to kill despite not being hungry. It is unknown what impact castration/neutering has on hunting behavior.

Cats frequently play with their catch even though they can quickly dispatch it with a bite to the neck (thereby severing or crushing the spinal cord). One theory suggests that play tires the prey, thus making it safer for the cat to kill it.

## Diet

Cats are neat eaters, rarely do they gulp down their food. Instead, they will sniff and approach it at various angles and then taste. Cats eat a wide variety of foods. As a predator, cats' primary diet consists of mammals, but birds can constitute 20% of their diet. Insectivores, such as moles, seem to be considered bad tasting to cats and are often killed but not eaten. One writer said that cats preferred house mice (*Mus musculus*) but showed distaste for deer mice (*Peromyscus spp.*). Cats also are hard on reptiles and crustaceans and are known to eat human food, carrion, and insects.

Cats eat grass for its ability to help them move their bowels or vomit.

## Resources

Baker, P. J., C. D. Soulsbury, G. Iossa, and S. Harris. 2010. Domestic Cat (*Felis catus*) and Domestic Dog (*Canis familiaris*) in *Urban Carnivores: Ecology, Conflict, and Conservation* edited by S. D. Gehrt, S. P.D. Riley, and B. L. Cypher. Baltimore: Johns Hopkins University Press, 157–171.

Caras, R. A. 1989. *A Cat is Watching: A Look at the Way Cats See Us.* New York, NY: Simon and Schuster.

Christiansen, P., and S. Wroe. 2007. Bite Forces and Evolutionary Adaptations to Feeding Ecology in Carnivores. *Ecology* 88:2(Feb):347–358.

Hartwell, S. 2000-2012. Cat Communication and Language. http://www.petpeoplesplace.com/resources/articles/cats/27-cat-communication-language_7.htm visited Oct 16, 2012.

National Possum Control Agencies. 2009. Feral and Stray Cats: Monitoring and Control, a Preliminary Guideline Towards Good Practice. Wellington, NZ: National Possum Control Agencies.

Necker, Claire. 1970. *The Natural History of Cats.* Cranbury, NJ: A. S. Barnes and Co., Inc.

Robertson, S. A. 2007. Review Article: A Review of Feral Cat Control. *Journal of Feline Medicine and Surgery* 10:366-375.

Robley, A., D. Purdey, M. Johnston, M. Lindeman, F. Busana, and K. Long. 2007. Experimental Trials to Determine Effective Fence Designs for Feral Cat and Fox Exclusion. *Ecological Management & Restoration* 8:3(Dec):193-198.

Scott, K. C., J. K. Levy, and C. Crawford. 2002. Characteristics of Free-roaming Cats Evaluated in a Trap-neuter-return Program. *Journal of the American Veterinary Medical Association* 221:8(October 15):1136-1138.

Turner, D. C. and P. Bateson (eds). *The Domestic Cat: The Biology of Its Behavior.* 2nd ed. Cambridge, UK: Cambridge Press.

Yahoo Answers. 2012. What feeling is expressed by a cat with its ears flat on its head? http://uk.answers.yahoo.com/question/index?qid=20090807122157AALVj9o Visited November 12, 2012.

Chapter 3. **Safety Risks**

Control of house cats involves legal, physical, and biological risks. When all three elements are combined, they form what I call the "Risk Triad" (Fig. 1). I have already touched on one of the legal land-mines that can confront anyone seeking to control house cats. I will not say anything more about that other than beware, consult appropriate authorities, and be sure of your legal standing before performing any control of cats. But I will discuss legal issues involved in running a control service.

This chapter will deal with the other two risks—the physical and biological risks that confront controllers of cats. These risks can occur during the inspection process as well as the physical handling of cats, be it directly or in traps. You must keep these issues (and others) in mind to protect yourself from injury and death. To review: **physical risks include** falls, cuts, scrapes, bites, scratches, bumping head, and vehicle accidents, while **biological risks include** histoplasmosis, rabies, *Baylisascaris procyonis*, other zoonotic diseases, and even include infections that can be contracted from interacting with the public and customers.

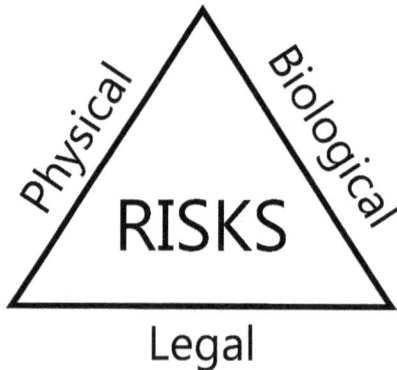

**Fig. 1.** *The risk triad.*

**Evaluating Risk**

The level of risk you will be exposed to is influenced by several factors, including: frequency of exposure, duration of exposure, and severity of consequences. Safety is determined by personal protection equipment and your behavior. Always keep in mind that while you can control your behavior, you can't control the behavior of the animals, the environment, or even other people. Control of vertebrates is dangerous and potentially life-threatening. What follows is a review of some of the most important risks you face. It is by no means a complete list.

If you have any concerns about your safety, I strongly recommend you hire a qualified professional before performing control of cats.

## Physical Safety

Animal control sometimes requires you go off the beaten path, where boards, nails, uneven ground etc. all pose risks to your physical well-being. Ankles can twist, nails can puncture feet, cuts and scrapes can be sustained. Be aware of your surroundings. It is easy to be so concerned about your task that you don't look where you are walking and thereby walk off an embankment (Fig. 2).

Wear quality work gloves and don clothing suitable for the conditions in which you will be working. At minimum, this should include, leather work gloves, long-sleeved shirts and long pants.

**Fig. 2.** *Stepping backwards to view the entire roof, could result in a very bad fall off this retaining wall.*

Shoes should protect the foot completely. No flip flops. Additional suggestions, can be found below.

**Criminal Assault.** Charles Holt of Ohio mentions the risk of being a victim of criminal assault. He is quite correct to note that wildlife control operators (WCOs) drive to addresses almost without question. While impossible to protect yourself from an ambush attack (as demonstrated by the September 2010 murder of Chris Taylor who was delivering pizza in Omaha, NE), it would be prudent to be careful. If you feel uncomfortable around a client or in a particular location, it could be that your instincts are telling you something. Holt suggests that you make sure someone always knows where you are going. In addition, remember that your equipment, such as flashlight or multi-purpose tool could be used to save your life. Also keep in mind that free-range cat proponents can be quite passionate in their protection of cats. So while you are controlling cats, be aware of your surroundings. Even if you are controlling cats on your own property, be aware of surroundings.

## Disease Safety

Diseases are contracted through various means. The ones below are the most important and common facing those that work with free-range animals. You can contract diseases through:
- Inhalation (breathing),
- Injection (bites, including insect bites),
- Ingestion (eating or drinking), and
- Absorption (scratches in skin, contact with mucosa).

Given these 4 routes for infection, it is easy to consider how to protect yourself by employing barriers and sanitary practices to increase the difficulty for infectious material to access you via these routes. In short, wear your protective clothing. The amount of protective equipment you should wear is directly related to the level of potential exposure.

In low risk situations, such as setting traps in a back yard, you will only need gloves, long-sleeved shirt, long pants, and good shoes. Depending on the time of year, insect repellent to protect against ticks and mosquitoes is advisable also.

In higher risk situations, such as fecal clean-outs or entering in crawl spaces (be sure to consult Occupational Health and Safety Administration for guidance on safety in enclosed spaces), you should consider wearing additional protective equipment, including Tyvek®

body suit with hood and booties, nitrile gloves, mouth-nose respirator (N-100), though a full-face mask is preferable. Be sure you are fit-tested and receive training regarding the use of respirators prior to wearing one.

You should also ensure that your tetanus vaccination is up to date.

The second step is personal hygiene. Washing your hands, said one veterinarian, will protect you from many risks. Since hand washing is difficult in the field, carry and use waterless hand sanitizers. They should have at least 60% alcohol to be effective. Sanitizers with cloth may be even more effective as the scrubbing action will help to remove organic material that holds germs.

Changing your clothes and taking a shower before hugging your children can reduce the risk of exposing your family to zoonotics. Inspect yourself for ticks and any bites.

Carry a first-aid kit (Fig. 3) so you can quickly treat minor cuts and scrapes with appropriate antiseptic ointments and cover them with a bandage. Remember, your skin is your first line of defense against a number of infectious agents.

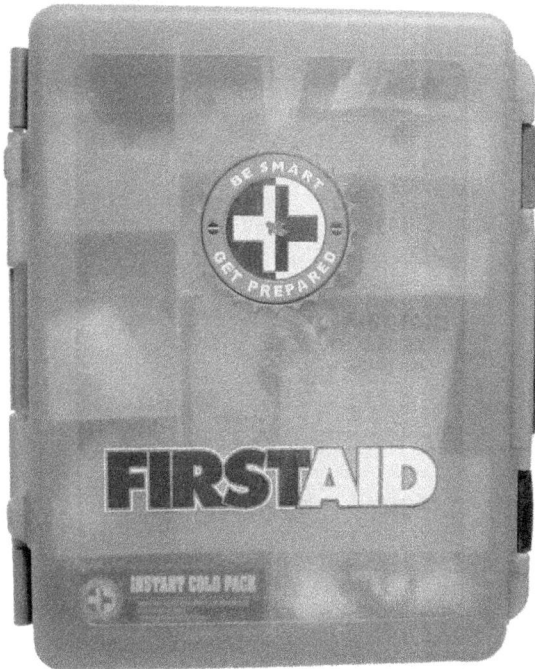

**Fig. 3.** *A first-aid kit plays an important role in keeping you healthy.*

## *If you are bitten by a cat,*
## *contact medical professionals right away.*

Finally, monitor your own health. Most zoonotic infections manifest themselves through fever and body aches within 2 to 3 weeks of exposure. Just because you think it is human flu, don't forget that it might be something else. Tell your doctor each and every time you meet that you work with wildlife. I would recommend carrying a card (Fig. 3a) to remind you and medical personnel of the common diseases you can encounter. If you don't, your physician might not think of zoonotic infections.

Be prudent, not paranoid. Remember that people have hunted and trapped animals for centuries with no ill effects. Even if mistakes are made, the odds of an infection occurring are remote. You, however, should strive to reduce risks whenever possible.

---

**U.S. Department of Agriculture**
**Animal and Plant Health Inspection Service**
**Medical Alert Card**

This employee may be working cooperatively or in a volunteer status for other agencies, as a contractor in concert with USDA APHIS surveillance programs, or USDA APHIS emergency programs. The medical information provided on the reverse of this card is to aid in their diagnosis and treatment of potential illness incurred while in the performance of those assignments. The employee bearing this card must provide appropriate identification and this card to aid in diagnosis and treatment.
The bearer of this card is advised to make available appropriate identification and status of coverage for medical/workers' compensation insurance at the time of seeking aid.

**APHIS FORM 260a  (DEC 2007)**             **See Reverse Side**

---

**ATTENTION MEDICAL PERSONNEL**

This employee is likely to be exposed to pesticides and certain zoonotic diseases which are not routinely considered in the differential diagnosis of febrile illnesses. APHIS requests that you consider pesticide poisoning and the following diseases in case of serious illness in this individual:

**Highly Pathogenic Avian Influenza, Anthrax, Monkeypox, Q Fever, Hantavirus, Plague, Rocky Mountain Spotted Fever, Leptospirosis, Tularemia, Lyme Disease, Brucellosis, Typhus, Arbovirus Encephalitis** (Eastern, Western, St. Louis, California), **Giardiasis, Histoplasmosis, Psittacosis, Spirochaetal Relapsing Fever, Bovine Tuberculosis, and West Nile Virus.**

APHIS FORM 260a (Reverse)

**Fig. 3a.** *This medical alert card is carried by USDA-Wildlife Services personnel.*

**Fig. 4.** *Wasp investigating crack by this doorbell.*

### Biological Risks

**Animal Attacks.** One of the risks in inspecting areas for wildlife is that you may in fact directly encounter them. While most animals, particularly cats, avoid humans by either fleeing or hiding, there is always the possibility that one may attack.

During your inspection or work, you may encounter other risks such as bees or hornets. Hornets and wasps tend to build nests on structures in areas with protection from rain (Fig. 4). Hornets can also build nests in the ground.

Brown recluse spiders and their tendency to hide in attics and crawl spaces make them a potential threat to individuals performing inspections.

**Plants.** Watch out for poison ivy (Fig. 5), poison oak (Fig. 6), and sumac (Fig. 7). The primary symptom is a rash caused by the skin reacting to the oil in the plant. If exposed, wash exposed skin with soap and water immediately being careful not to spread the oils to other parts of the body. Different people have different reactions and that sensitivity to the oil can change as you age.

**Fig. 5.** *The saying goes, "If leaves be 3, let it be." Poison ivy can occur in plant, shrub, and vine forms.*

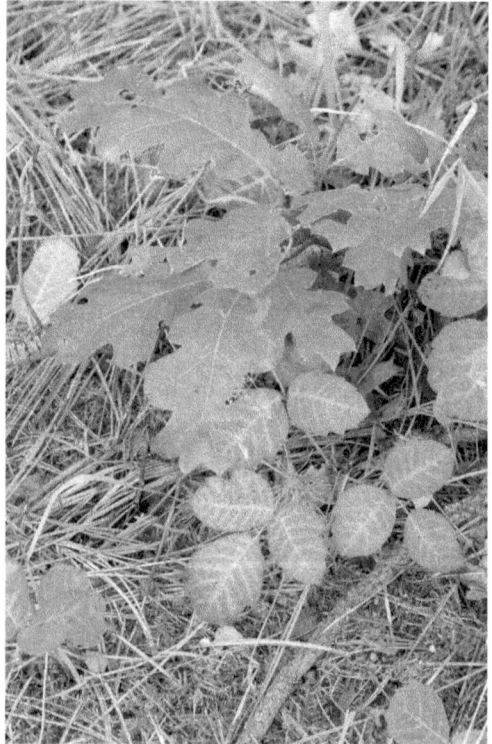

**Fig. 6.** *Poison oak (below) with tree oak (upper). Photo courtesy of <u>www. poison-ivy.org</u>.*

**Fig. 7.** *Poison sumac. Photo courtesy of www.poison-ivy.org.*

### Diseases Threatening Humans

Cats, like all animals, are subject to a number of diseases. Infectious diseases fall into various classes: viral, rickettsial, bacterial, protozoal, fungal, helminth, and prion. I will only focus on those diseases that pose risk to human-interests. Keep in mind that the following list is NOT complete and that cats can pose disease risk to domestic and wild animals.

### VIRAL DISEASES

### Rabies

**Infectious agent.** Rabies is a viral disease that infects the central nervous systems of mammals and humans.

**Hosts.** Any mammal can contract the disease. Species most commonly associated with rabies include bats, raccoons, skunks, coyotes, and foxes. However, the CDC noted that rabies amongst cats rose from 294 cases in 2008 to 300 in 2009. While it may not seem like many rabid cats, you must understand that cats are more likely to come into contact with owners.

**Transmission.** Bites and contact with infected saliva on open wounds are the most common form of transmission. Inhalation also is possible, such as bat-inhabited caves. The rabies virus can remain infectious in a carcass until decomposition is well advanced.

**Symptoms.** The initial symptoms of rabies mimic other viral infections, including fever, headache, malaise, and disorders of the upper respiratory and gastrointestinal tracts.

**Treatment.** Preventative vaccine or post exposure shots. Vaccine recipients may still require additional shots after a bite. Once clinical symptoms of rabies have appeared, death is likely. Therefore, it is important to receive medical diagnosis and treatments quickly if exposure was possible.

**Prevention.** Avoid being bitten or exposure to brain or nervous system tissues.

## RICKETTSIAL DISEASES

### Rocky Mountain Spotted Fever

**Infectious agent.** *Rickettsia rickettsii*
**Host.** Rodents.
**Transmission.** A tick bite, including the American dog tick (*Dermacentor variabilis*), Rocky Mountain wood tick (*Dermacentor andersoni*), and brown dog tick (*Rhipicephalus sanguineus)*. Cat flea can also transmit the disease.
**Symptoms.** Fever, headache, abdominal pain, vomiting, and muscle pain. A rash also may develop, but is often absent for the first few days, and in some patients, never develops.
**Treatment.** Antibiotics
**Prevention.** Avoid tick habitat, wear light clothes, use tick repellents, tuck pants into socks, inspect for ticks.

## BACTERIAL DISEASES

### Lyme Disease

**Infectious agent.** A spirochete bacterium called *Borrelia burgdorferi*.
**Host.** Many organisms but the white-footed mouse (*Peromyscus leucopus*) is a key host.
**Transmission.** Deer tick bites, particularly those at the nymph stage.
**Symptoms.** Bull's-eye-shaped rashes, ~5 inches in diameter occur in most infections (Fig. 8). Flu-like symptoms common in early stages of disease.
**Treatment.** Antibiotics are effective provided they are administered soon enough.

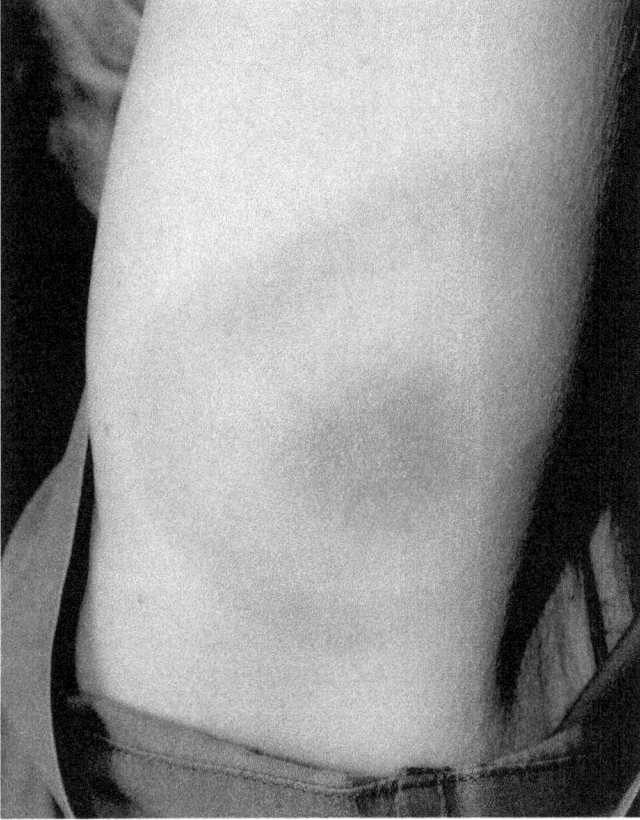

**Fig. 8.** *Bull's-eye rash that occurs with 80% of Lyme disease infections. Photo by CDC/James Gathany.*

**Prevention**. Avoid tick habitat, wear light clothes, use tick repellents, tuck pants into socks, inspect for ticks.

*Note:* There is a new disease called STARI (Southern Tick Associated Rash Illness). STARI presents symptoms similar to those of Lyme disease but it is not caused by the Lyme disease bacterium. The lone star tick (Fig. 9) (*Amblyomma americanum*) is a vector for STARI and can be found as far north as Maine and west as Texas and Nebraska.

**Fig. 9.** *Lone star tick in questing position looking for a host. Photo by James Gathany of the CDC.*

### Plague

**Infectious agent.** *Yersinia pestis.*

**Host.** Ground squirrels and the fleas that reside on them. Cat flea (*Ctenocephalides felis*).

**Transmission.** Fleas. They will leave their dead host and search for new hosts. Outbreaks of fleas can be substantial. Scratches, bites, and other forms of contact with infected cats.

**Symptoms.** High fever 103 to 106°F, headache, fatigue, nausea, changes in heart rate and altered consciousness. Enlarged lymph node(s) (¾-inch wide) may be present also.

**Treatment.** Antibiotics.

**Prevention.** Avoid getting bitten or scratched by cats. Infection can occur when caring for or in face to face contact with infected cats. Wear gloves and other protective equipment when handling them and remember that cats can carry the fleas capable of transmitting plague. Plague tends to be endemic in the western states, so cat trappers from those regions should be especially careful.

### Cat Bites

**Infectious agent.** Multitude of bacteria.
**Host.** Cat.
**Transmission.** Cat bite.
**Symptoms.** Swelling, redness, oozing, fever, and other signs of infection.
**Treatment.** Antibiotics rapidly administered.
**Prevention.** Avoid being bitten by cats.

### Cat Scratch Fever

**Infectious agent.** *Bartonella henselae.*
**Hosts.** Cats typically do not present any symptoms.
**Transmission.** Bites and/or scratches from cats, their fleas, and lice.
**Symptoms.** Bite or scratch site may be infected. Lymph nodes, especially those around the head, neck, and upper limbs, become swollen. Additionally, a person with cat scratch disease may experience fever, headache, fatigue, and a poor appetite. Rare complications of *B. henselae* infection include bacillary angiomatosis and Parinaud's oculolandular syndrome. Immuno-compromised individuals at greatest risk.
**Treatment.** Various medications are available.
**Prevention.** Avoid scratches and bites from cats and their fleas. Do not allow cats to lick wounds.


## PROTOZOAL DISEASES

### Toxoplasmosis

**Infectious Agent.** *Toxoplasma gondii.*
**Host.** Cats are the primary host.
**Transmission.** Eggs are shed in cat feces which can then contaminate soil, food, or water. Eggs can remain viable for up to 18 months. Eggs are ingested. No evidence that the infection is transmitted through bites. However, one study found that owners bitten by their own cats had a higher prevalence of antibodies to *Toxplasma gondii* than those bitten by a foreign cat.
**Symptoms.** For healthy people, there may be no symptoms associated with infection but research is growing about the effects of sub-clinical infection. Individuals suffering from immune deficiencies can develop severe infections. Pregnant women can pass the infection to their unborn children.

**Fig. 10.** *Personal protective equipment to help protect against zoonotic diseases. Note that full-face mask (not pictured) is recommended.*

**Treatment.** Persons who are ill can be treated with a combination of drugs such as pyrimethamine and sulfadiazine, plus folinic acid.

**Prevention.** One study found that there was no difference between infection rates of indoor vs. outdoor cats. Cover sand boxes and fence garden areas to prevent use by cats. Avoiding areas contaminated by cat droppings unless wearing protective equipment, including gloves (Fig. 10). Full-face mask is recommended (not pictured).

### Cat Roundworm

**Infectious Agent.** *Toxocara cati* (CDC *Toxocaris* 2011)
**Host.** Cats
**Transmission.** Ingesting eggs from fecally contaminated soil.
**Symptoms.** Most infected people lack symptoms. Those that do show symptoms exhibit fever, coughing, enlarged liver or pneumonia or inflammation of the eye.
**Treatment.** Antiparasitic and anti-inflamation drugs.
**Prevention.** Avoid ingesting contaminated food and soil. Clean up pet feces. Wash hands.

### Diseases Threatening Other Animals

*Toxoplasma gondii* has been implicated in killing southern sea otters off the coast of California.

Cats can also carry *Sarcosystis neurona,* the infectious agent behind equine protozoal myeloencephalitis that can kill horses. Though opossum feces are the primary vector, cats can be one of the numerous intermediate hosts.

## Resources

I would like to acknowledge the following for information contained in this chapter namely Chris Anchor, Charles Holt, Mike Page, and CDC.gov. Thanks to Tim Hiller, a Wildlife Research Scientist, from Salem, OR for his careful review.

Baker, P. J., C. D. Soulsbury, G. Iossa, and S. Harris. 2010. Domestic Cat (*Felis catus*) and Domestic Dog (*Canis familiaris*) in *Urban Carnivores: Ecology, Conflict, and Conservation* edited by S. D.

Gehrt, S.P.D. Riley, and B. L. Cypher. Baltimore: Johns Hopkins University Press, 157-171.

CDC [Centers for Disease Control]. 1998. Compendium of Measures to Control *Chlamydia psittaci* Infection Among Humans (Psittacosis) and Pet Birds (Avian Chlamydiosis), 1998. *Morbity and Mortality Weekly Report,* 47:No.RR-10(July 10):1-19.

CDC. 2010. Parasites — Toxoplasmosis (*Toxoplasma* infection): Treatment. http://www.cdc.gov/parasites/toxoplasmosis/treatment.html Updated November 2. Visited on August 19, 2012.

CDC. 2011. The Burden of Rabies. http://www.cdc.gov/Features/dsRabies/ updated September 28, 2011. Visited on August 19, 2012.

CDC. 2011. Cat Scratch Disease. http://www.cdc.gov/healthypets/diseases/catscratch.htm Last updated June 23, 2011. Visited on August 19, 2012.

CDC. 2011. Parasites — Toxocariasis (also known as Roundworm Infection). http://www.cdc.gov/parasites/toxocariasis/prevent.html Last updated on November 2, 2011. Visited August 19, 2012.

Corpus, L. D., and K. M. Corpus. 1991. Mass Flea Outbreak at a Child Care Facility: Case Report. *American Journal of Public Health* 81:4(Apr):497-498.

Davidson, W. R. editor. 2006. *Field Manual of Wildlife Diseases in the Southeastern United States.* Third edition. Athens, GA: Southeastern Cooperative Wildlife Disease Cooperative.

Duara, N. and S. Dubois. 2012. Plague Confirmed in Oregon Man Bitten by a Stray Cat. Associated Press. Portland, OR. June 15.

Frenkel, J. K. 1973. Toxoplasma in and around us. *BioScience,* 23:343-352.

Gage, K. L., D. T. Dennis, K. A. Orloski, P. Ettestad, T. L. Brown, P. J. Reynolds, W. J. Pape, C. L. Fritz, L. G. Carter, and J. D. Stein. 2000. Cases of Cat-Associated Human Plague in the Western US, 1977-1998. *Clinical Infectious Diseases* 30:6(June):893-900.

Kaiser, R. M., R. L. Garman, M. G. Bruce, R. S. Weyant, and D. A. Ashford. 2002. Clinical Significance and Epidemiology of NO-1, an Unusual Bacterium Associated with Dog and Cat Bites. *Emerging Infectious Diseases* 8:2(February). http://www.nc.cdc.gov/eid/article/8/2/01-0139.htm

*Liebeck v. McDonald's Restaurants, P.T.S., Inc.,* No. D-202 CV-93-02419, 1995 WL 360309 (Bernalillo County, N.M. Dist. Ct. August

18, 1994), docket entry from nmcourts.com accessed on December 16, 2011 from Wikipedia.

Metzger, M. 2001. Public Health: Wild Rodents + Fleas = Risky Business. *Pest Control Magazine,* (Feb):28-31.

Mora, Jacki. 2011. http://www.kmtv.com/news/local/135252693.html. (Dec 8) visited January 5, 2012.

Robertson, S.A. 2007. Review Article: A Review of Feral Cat Control. *Journal of Feline Medicine and Surgery* 10:366-375.

The Wildlife Society. 2011. Toxoplasmosis in Feral Cats: Health Risks to Humans and Wildlife. January. 2pp.

Wrestling, K., C. Jorup-Ronstrom, and B. Evengard. 2010. Toxoplasmosis not transmitted by cat bites, but high antibodies to *Toxoplasma gondii* in patients bitten by their own cat. *Scandinavian Journal of Infectious Diseases* 42:687-690.

# Chapter 4. Damage Identification

## Determining Cat Numbers

Identification of cat damage in most circumstances is relatively straight forward. Clients will often relate sightings of cats and may even have an idea on approximate numbers. The challenge for those interested in controlling cats is how to determine the number of cats present. More concretely, how do you know you have them all?

How many cats can there be? Unfortunately, no simple and foolproof method exists for accurately and completely estimating cat numbers. Studies have shown that cats numbers can reach population densities greater than $100/km^2$ only when they are fed. So you can use that number as an upper limit. What follows is a listing of techniques to help you estimate the proper number of cats. Use these techniques cautiously and err on the side of believing that you have likely not seen them all.

If you are in the business of removing cats, you must determine if your client requires 100% removal of the cat population or whether he/she will be satisfied with less than complete removal. The larger the area and the greater the number of cats to be removed, the harder it is to obtain a complete, or what is known as an absolute, census. You may only be able to develop a relative census meaning you have an approximation of the number of cats in the area.

## Option 1. Sightings

This technique is effective at noting presence but it is time intensive. Sightings can be done at feeding stations. It can be helpful to use a camera with a 300 mm lens or greater to help you count and identify individual cats back at the office. Cats not habituated to human presence (e.g. cat feeders) have a lower chance of being seen. Sightings by clients should also be used to determine estimates but use caution on how much you rely on them. Whether you perform cat counts on your own or interview the client, be sure to take any numbers of cats identified as the minimum number, not the maximum.

Sightings at night can be performed with the help of a strong spotlight (500,000 candles or higher). Scan the area looking for the green eye-shine of the cats (Fig. 1). In large land areas with intersecting roads, cats can be spotlighted from a motor vehicle. Just

**Fig. 1.** *Green eyeshine of cats.*

be sure one person drives while the passenger(s) spotlights and records. Detection probability begins to drop off after 22 yards and declines to a probability of 20% at 44 yards. If spotlighting would disturb people, perform surveys between 0600-0800 hours and between the hours of 1800-2000 hrs. Then calculate the sightings by number per road mile.

## Option 2. Track Traps

Track traps, as the name suggests consists of placing sooted-plates or sifted soil/sand where cats may step on them and leave a track. Position the track traps on trails and intersections every 100 yards. Check them daily. Some researchers use meat-baited tubes (e.g. PVC pipe) and place ink pads near the entrances with white paper in the middle so that tracks will be left. Just be sure that the overhang of the pipes are large enough to protect the pads and paper from the elements. Stake the pipe so it doesn't roll. One study left out plates for 200 night equivalents and obtained 1 track so its effectiveness is questionable.

Calculate the evidence as the number of individuals per square mile.

**Identifying House Cat Tracks.** Identifying tracks in the real world takes skill. I recommend everyone who wants to learn more about tracking should read anything by Jim Halfpenny or Mark Elbroch. Here are a few tips to identify cat tracks. Look carefully at Figures 2-4 and the Track Identification sidebar.

**Fig. 2.** *Tracks of a house cat.*

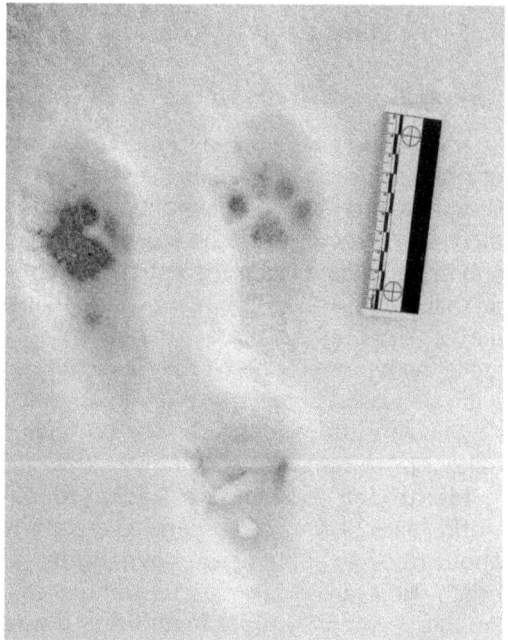

**Fig. 3.** *House cat track in snow (close up). Scale is in cm.*

**Fig. 4.** *House cat tracks in snow. Note, however, that this trail pattern is not distinctive to cats.*

## Option 3. Sandbox

Sandboxes exploit the cat's tendency to defecate in loose sand, like kitty litter. Creating sandboxes or areas containing kitty litter (just be sure to protect the latter from rain) can be checked for the presence of feces. The technique has its weaknesses. One study employed boxes for 560 nights and recovered no scats.

Calculate the evidence as the number of individuals per square mile.

# Cat Tracks

Tracks are relatively rare in human-impacted environments because of concrete, asphalt and compacted ground prevents the signature of a track. But when tracks are found, consider the inter-digit relationship between the heel and toe pads. The space in feline tracks forms a C (Fig. 1). Front track of the cat average 1½ inches in length and 1⅜ inches wide and 1⁵⁄₁₆ × 1⅜ inches respectively for the rear. Dog or canine tracks, in contrast, have space sufficient to allow you to draw an X in the inter-digit space (Fig. 2). Keep in mind that while most cats have 4 toes, sometimes they have 5.

**Resources:**

Cabrera, K.C. 2012. Domestic Cats. http://www.bear-tracker.com/domcat.html visited February 22, 2013.

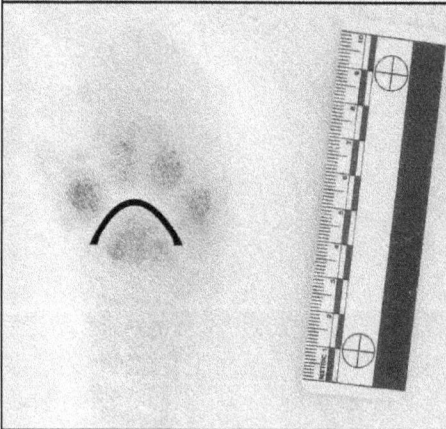

**Fig. 1.** Cat track. Note how the space between heel pad and toes forms a C.

**Fig. 2.** Dog track. Note how the space between the heel pad and the toes allow an X to be drawn.

**Fig. 5.** *Trail cameras can be quite useful.*

## Option 4. Trail cameras

Use in place of doing on-site counts. Choose cameras that can take night photos without visible flash (Figs. 5-6). Be sure to position cameras facing north so that the sun doesn't shine directly in the lens. Ensure that objects, like branches, that are likely to be moved by wind, are not in the sensor's view whenever possible. Normal sensitivity on the sensor should be sufficient.

Evaluate the images as the number of individuals per square mile.

Learn how to identify cats by photo. State wildlife biologists regularly receive photos from the public claiming that they have proof

**Fig. 6.** *Trail cameras can be quite helpful for night monitoring.*

mountain lions (*Puma concolor*) exist in the state. The vast majority of these images are actually bobcats (*Lynx rufus*) or house cats.

Table 1 contains some tips so you don't make the same mistake.

### Table 1. Distinguishing cats, bobcats, and mountain lions

| Sign | House cat | Bobcat | Mountain Lion |
|------|-----------|--------|---------------|
| Length | 18 inches | 3 ft | 7 to 8 ft |
| Track Width | 1.38 | 2.63 | 3 to 3.5 in |
| Tail | 12 inches; Longer than hind leg | Shorter than hind leg | ½ of body length |
| Color | Highly variable | Black spots | Tan |

### Identifying Cat Feeders

Knowing where the cats are being taken care of is essential in your cat control program. Feeders of free-range cats will help congregate cats in 1 location (at least for a short period of time) and also will compete with your ability to trap them.

Take a drive through the neighborhood. Look for houses with dishes outdoors, partially opened garage doors (Fig. 7) that will suggest someone is feeding free-range cats.

**Fig. 7.** *Partially opened garage doors are a dead giveaway for cats.*

**Fig. 8.** *Entrance used by cats to access the crawl space under a house-trailer.*

## Damage to Structures

Cat damage to structures tends to be limited to odors and destruction of soft items such as couches and insulation

**Fig. 9.** *Insulation in a subfloor that has been matted down by cats.*

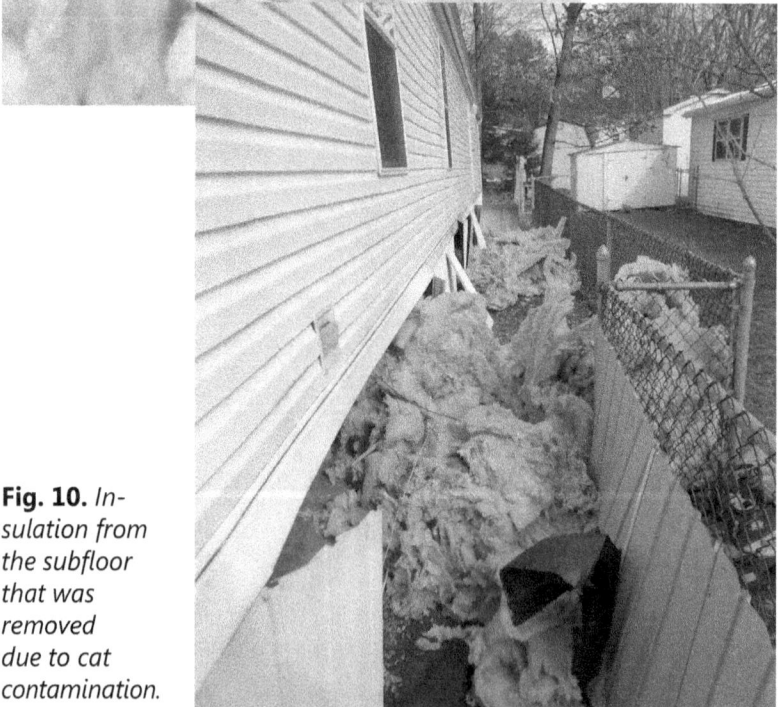

**Fig. 10.** *Insulation from the subfloor that was removed due to cat contamination.*

(Figs. 8-10). Unlike raccoons, cats lack the physical prowess to tear apart walls and dig. Cats urinate at a rate of 0.66 to 0.94 oz/2.2lbs of body weight. Though they urinate infrequently, it is concentrated and quite pungent.

**Cat Sign on Cars.** Cats are not known to damage cars. But they like to climb on them. Whether it is for the warmth of the engine or metal or the height advantage doesn't matter. Just be sure to check the vehicle for the tell-tale cat prints that may be present (Figs. 11-12).

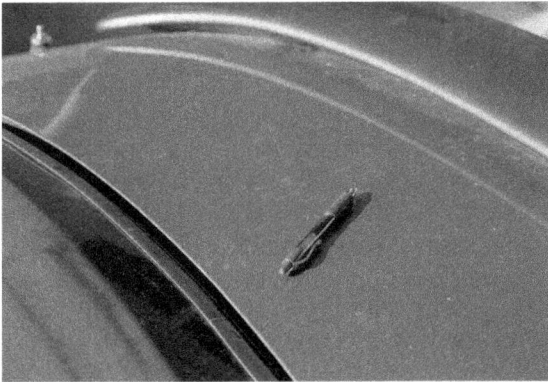

**Fig. 11.** *Cat prints on trunk of a car.*

**Fig. 12.** *Cat prints on the car's back window.*

**Damage to Animals/Pets**

As a rule cats tend to prey on animals that are about 1% of their own weight. Free-range cats only leave a small percentage of their captures at the owner's doorsteps. Up to 49% of prey were left at site. About 30% is eaten. Sometimes all that remains is a group of strewn feathers (Fig. 13).

To confirm the bird was alive, or still warm, when its feathers were plucked, look at the feather shaft at the point which would have attached to the bird's skin called the calamus (Fig. 14). If the calamus is clean and free of flesh then it was plucked from the bird while it was still alive. If it has a piece of flesh attached, then it was plucked after the bird was dead. It is reported that cats will bite off the wings of quail and discard them. Cats don't predate on eggs, but will take chicks.

Look at bones. Cats lack the crushing power of dogs and other canines. Instead, cats will use their canine teeth to scrape to shear meat or bone. Look for the resultant grooves in the bones.

To confirm cat predation, animals may be skinned to help expose the presence of canine punctures. Wear protective gloves and clothing (see Chapter 2). Pay particular attention to the neck region. Locate the puncture marks which could signify the canine teeth. Measure them. If they are beyond 21 mm apart or closer than 8.5mm, then it cannot be a cat.

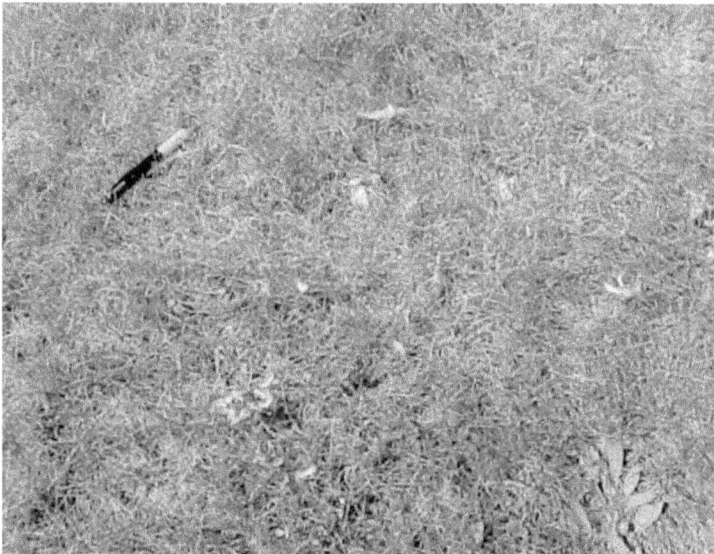

**Fig. 13.** *Strewn feathers can signify a predation site by cats.*

**Fig. 14.** *Feather with a clean calamus meaning it came from a bird while it was alive or still warm.*

### Damage to Gardens and Landscapes

**Fecal Pollution.** One study determined that 9,000 cats deposed 155,200 lbs of fecal material outdoors per year or 17.24 lbs/year/cat. Cats usually cover their scats deposited within their territories (Fig. 15) but will leave them uncovered elsewhere.

**Identifying Cat Scat.** Cat scat tends to be segmented ropes with blunt and pointed ends (Figs. 16-17) but can vary greatly depending on content. Some may describe the scat as "tootsie roll-like" in appearance. Hair is commonly found in cat scat. Generally, scat will be buried outdoors but may be visible at the extremes of "territories."

**Fig. 15.** *Toilette area where the cat(s) scraped the soil to cover the defecation/urination spot.*

**Fig. 16.** *Cat feces which it had placed in a small depression.*

**Fig. 17.** *Feline scats tend to be segmented cords with a point on one end.*

**Scratch Posts.** You might be able to identify scratch posts used by cats to mark territory and sharpen claws (Fig. 18). Using commercial scratch posts as a guide, scratches should be no higher than 30 to 32 inches. Cats tend to scratch trees with soft bark that exist along trails and paths.

**Noise Pollution.** Non-neutered male cats can be quite boisterous at night or particularly when fighting.

## Resources

Baker, P. J., C. D. Soulsbury, G. Iossa, and S. Harris. 2010. Domestic Cat (*Felis catus*) and Domestic Dog (*Canis familiaris*) in *Urban Carnivores: Ecology, Conflict, and Conservation* edited by S. D.

**Fig. 18.** *A scratch post could look like this.*

Gehrt, S. P.D. Riley, and B. L. Cypher. Baltimore: Johns Hopkins University Press, 157-171.

Cabrera, K. A. 2012. Domestic Cat. http://www.bear-tracker.com/domcat.html visited on Oct. 20, 2012.

Cabrera, K. A. 2012. Bobcat. http://www.bear-tracker.com/bobcat.html visited on Oct. 20, 2012.

Cats. 2012. *Wikipedia*. http://en.wikipedia.org/wiki/Cat visited on Oct. 26, 2012.

Coleman, J. S. and S. A. Temple. 1989. Effects of Free-Ranging Cats on Wildlife: A Progress Report. *Proceedings of the Fourth Eastern Wildlife Damage Control Conference.* 9-12.

Feldman, H. N. 1994. Methods of scent marking in the domestic cat. *Canadian Journal of Zoology* 72(6): 1093-1099.

Hawkins, C. C., W. E. Grant, and M. T. Longnecker. Effect of house cats, being fed in parks, on California birds and rodents. 2004. *Proceedings 4th International Urban Wildlife Symposium.* Shaw et al., eds. Pages 164-170. http://cals.arizona.edu/pubs/adjunct/snr0704/snr07042l.pdf.

Lloyd, K. A., S. Hernandez, G. Marshall, K. Abernathy, and B. Foster. 2012. A Day in the Life of a Traveling Feline: New Technology to Track Free-Roaming Domestic Cats. *Wildlife Professional* 6:3(Summer):60-1.

Missouri Department of Conservation. http://mdc.mo.gov/discover-nature/wildlife-sightings/mountain-lions/description-and-signs visited 8/3/2012.

Necker, Claire. 1970. *The Natural History of Cats.* Cranbury, NJ: A. S. Barnes and Co., Inc.

National Possum Control Agencies. 2009. Feral and Stray Cats: Monitoring and Control, a Preliminary Guideline Towards Good Practice. Wellington, NZ: National Possum Control Agencies.

Ratz, H., H. Moller, and D. Fletcher. 1999. Predator Identification from Bite Marks on Penguin and Albatross Chicks. *Marine Ornithology.* 27:149-156.

Robertson, S. A. 2007. Review Article: A Review of Feral Cat Control. *Journal of Feline Medicine and Surgery* 10:366-375.

Schmidt, P. M., B. L. Pierce, and R. R. Lopez. 2007. Estimating Free-roaming Cat Densities in Urban Areas: Comparison of Mark Re-sight and Distance Sampling. *Wildl. Biol. Pract.,* 3:1(July):18-27.

Sterba, J. 2012. *Nature Wars: The Incredible Story of How Wildlife Comebacks Turned Backyards in Battlegrounds.* NY, NY: Crown Publishers.

Vantassel. S. M. 2012. *Wildlife Damage Inspection Handbook,* 3rd ed. Lincoln, NE: Wildlife Control Consultant.

*WikiAnswers.com.* What is the average length of a cat? http://wiki.answers.com/Q/What_is_the_average_length_of_a_cat visited Oct 7, 2012.

# Chapter 5. **Less-Lethal Control Techniques**

The term less-lethal may come as a surprise to many who are familiar with traditional dichotomy of non-lethal and lethal control methods. I have written elsewhere that such a dichotomy is actually false because many so-called non-lethal techniques actually result in the death of animals.

## Habitat Modification

"If you remove it, they will go." My quote is the reverse of the famous quote in *Field of Dreams*—"If you build it, they will come." High numbers of free-range and feral cats can only occur when humans permit it. Colonies, those consisting of 3 or more cats, can remain at a location only as long as the food holds out. The fact is feral cat colonies survive because humans feed and protect them. The feral cat lobby likes to assert a theory known as the "vacuum effect." This theory says that when cats are removed from an environment, other cats will simply move in from the surrounding area and "fill the void" that was created. Thus, it is argued, removal of cats doesn't actually reduce the problem, but rather sets up a cycle of control, refill, control, refill.

Though the theory is propounded with great vigor, the fact is its persuasive power crumbles upon closer scrutiny. First, the theory assumes that there are cats just waiting in the wings for a "gap" to appear so they can fill it. Second, it assumes that landowners will not remove the conditions that were favorable for the presence of cats in the first place. For example, if people were feeding cats and providing shelter, then it is understandable that the reproductive capacity of cats may outproduce efforts at population reduction.

But it would be silly to just focus on population control without spending any effort on removal of food and harborage. Wise cat control requires effort to remove the food and shelter available to cats. If food and shelter are gone, then why would a cat want to "fill the gap?" It would be like a renter wanting to live on a concrete slab. Third, the theory assumes that cats will refill the gap faster than the cats can be removed.

Habitat modification involves removing food, water, and shelter that can be used by cats. Food is probably the easiest to control. One

**Fig. 1.** *Cat being fed outdoors.*

publication says to remove cat access to old buildings and foundations and remove brush and piles of debris, and anything else that can provide shelter and cover to cats. Vegetation should be cut short as this will reduce the environment to conducive for small rodents.

Ordinances should be established to eliminate the feeding of cats. One of the ways to accomplish this is to invoke the principle of liability. Some communities have enacted rules stating if you feed the cat, you own the cat. Therefore, if the cat bites someone, transmits diseases, liability will incur on the feeder. Research does suggest that fed cats have increased survival and reproductive rates.

Unfortunately, few municipalities have the courage to enact ordinances regulating the feeding of cats. One report estimated that 22% of households in the U.S. feed outdoor cats that they do not own. Nevertheless, this method should be attempted, and attempted regularly until it is passed. In the meantime, all trash and garbage receptacles should be kept covered. Cats will feed on human garbage. Keep in mind; it is rare that reductions in the availability of food will be sufficient to eliminate the presence of cats. So keep your expectations reasonable. But the benefit of reducing food availability is the way it stresses the cats that remain. Not only will lack of food reduce their reproductive rate or success, it also makes the cats more vulnerable to control techniques mentioned below.

**Fig. 2.** *Community regulations against feeding can be quite helpful in reduction in cat numbers.*

Water is perhaps the most difficult to control. Lawn sprinklers, puddles, ponds, and streams can provide ample water for free-range and feral cats. However, anything that can be done to reduce water availability can be a big help, particularly in parts of the country that are already water stressed, like the southwest.

Removal of shelter is another key element. Cats need protection from the elements especially in environments that experience temperature extremes. Abandoned buildings, broken skirts of mobile homes, brush piles, and sheltered areas, should be removed or secured (see exclusion below) to prevent access. Again, it will be rare that enough locations will (or can) be addressed to eliminate the feral cat problem. The point is to place stress on the members of the colony, reduce their numbers, and make them more vulnerable to more direct forms of control.

## Exclusion

Exclusion refers to techniques designed to keep cats out of designated areas. Exclusion falls in 2 categories, protecting structures and protecting landscapes.

**Protecting Structures.** Any integrated cat control program requires preventing cats from access to protected resting areas provided by decks, porches, sheds, and crawl spaces. Fortunately, cats lack the leg and bite strength of raccoons, which can rip and tear into such areas. Even if cats are not living on your property, preventing their access to sheltered areas makes it more difficult for them to launch ambush attacks against native wildlife.

Half-inch galvanized hardware cloth secured with wide-headed screws or by using washers with your screws (to ensure the head doesn't slip through the mesh) is more than adequate to protect crawl space entries and openings. I suggest, however, that exclusion be strong enough to exclude skunks and woodchucks, as it only takes a little more effort to accomplish this. Simply bury the mesh 3 to 6 inches below the soil surface and bend it out at a 90° angle for 12 or more inches. This mesh skirt will help prevent skunks and woodchucks from digging under the mesh to gain access to the space. Add crushed limestone on ground to create a tighter interlocking surface to resist digging by other animals.

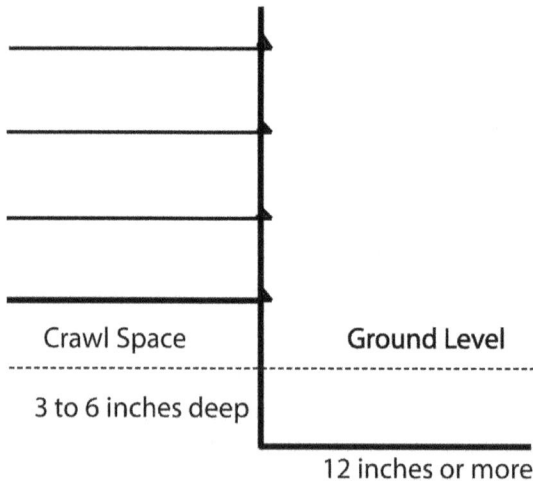

|                      |              |
|----------------------|--------------|
| Crawl Space          | Ground Level |
| 3 to 6 inches deep   |              |
|                      | 12 inches or more |

**Fig. 3.** *Trench-screen to prevent cat entry in a crawl space.*

**Fig. 4.** *Two-inch Dig DeFence® rods installed.*

Another option to prevent access is to hammer rebar or DIG De-fence® rods to exclude cats from crawling under decks and fences. Spacing between bars should not be more than 2 inches. Always consult Dig Safe® or other agencies involved with managing under-ground utilities prior to installation of any subterranean device.

**Protecting Landscapes.** Preventing cats from access to yards and gardens is more difficult than excluding them from structures. Not only is the cost likely to be higher, but many people will complain about the awful looking fencing needed to keep the cats out.

Fences used to exclude cats are either non-electric or electric. Non-electric fences require less maintenance and will often not run afoul of ordinances preventing the use of electric fences. Those living in areas with upkeep rules should consult officials about whether fences are permitted by the board. One study found that fences to exclude feral cats should be 71 inches tall and have an overhang of at least 24 inches that is curved with the curved end at least 17.75 inches from the vertical fence. It is possible that the overhang could be left as floppy.

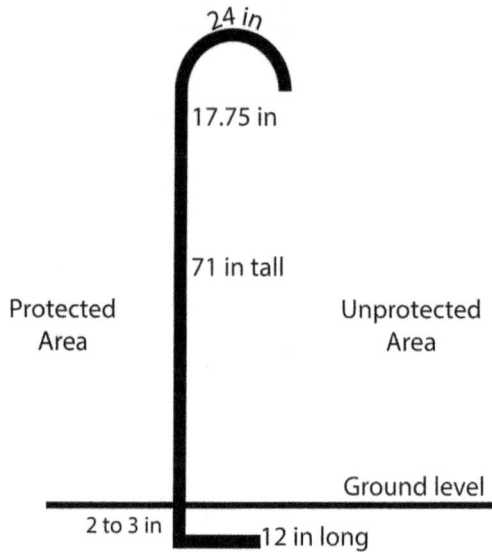

**Fig. 5.** *Side view of fence to keep cats out of a yard or garden.*

Ground skirt to prevent digging should be at least 12 inches and buried only a few inches below the soil or pinned securely so it can't be lifted up. It also should be galvanized to prevent decay and secured to posts.

If you already have a fence, you can investigate "cat spikes." These are plastic bluntly pointed spikes designed to prevent cats from stepping on them. I suspect they could also be useful in a garden, as cats wouldn't want to step on them there either.

### Frightening Devices

Frightening devices are non-chemical devices designed to scare animals from a particular location. Frightening devices are great in theory but frequently fail to achieve long-term results. The reasons are simple. Animals such as cats are exposed to a variety of noises and sounds. If new noises or disturbances caused cats to run away, how could cats living in urban areas ever survive? Second, animals habituate or become accustomed to novel experiences that are repeated and not accompanied with negative reinforcement.

Nevertheless, frightening devices can be helpful over the short-term. The best frightening devices are ones that only activate when the cats are present and that can be implemented to appear "new" to cats.

**Fig. 6.** *Woodstream® Havahart Spray Away™ Elite.*

The following are products sold that may be useful in frightening cats. Please note that I have not found peer-reviewed or peer-edited information on the effectiveness of these products. So buyer beware.

Scat Mat® is a pad that shocks the cat that steps on it. It is only suitable for indoor use. Use with caution if children are present. Cat-Stop® is a motion-activated device that emits an ultrasonic sound that purportedly scares cats.

Motion-activated sprinklers (Fig. 6) like the ScareCrow® or the Woodstream Spray Away™ (Fig. 6) may be helpful. Don't use when temperatures approach freezing.

## Repellents

Repellents are chemicals which can cause an aversive reaction to organisms without causing death. While a great idea, repellents frequently fail with mammals, including cats. The reasons are simple. Cats are exposed to a whole host of chemicals and odors. Second, if a cat finds something annoying, it can simply walk by the annoying smell or substance.

The Environmental Protection Agency has registered several repellents for cats. Olfactory repellents (those that repel by smell) include Methyl nonyl ketone, coyote and fox urine, thymol, black pepper oils, and oil of mustard.

Taste repellents include capsaicin, and denatonium saccharide.

Sometimes manufacturers combine chemicals in an attempt to achieve the benefits of taste and odor repellency.

While repellents rarely work the way the public wishes them to, there are a couple of situations and settings where repellents can be helpful. First, if a cat is gnawing on something such as wires, a taste repellent can be effective. Some online bulletin boards have claimed that sprays have also worked to stop cats from urinating against buildings. These may be worth a try, but I am skeptical.

Always read and follow the label instructions carefully. The label is the law. Do not apply these products on another's property without having the appropriate licenses with the state's pesticide board.

## Biological Controls

Dogs, especially aggressive ones, can be successful in keeping cats out of a given area. Larger dogs can even predate on cats.

## Resources

Fitzwater, W. D. Feral Cats. In: *Prevention and Control of Wildlife Damage*. Editors, Scott E. Hygnstrom, Robert M. Timm, Gary E. Larson. 1994. University of Nebraska-Lincoln. 2 vols.

Kelly Solutions. 2000. Nebraska Department of Agriculture Pesticide Registrations "Cats." http://www.kellysolutions.com/NE/show-productsbypest.asp?Pest_ID=VKKFAAA01 Last updated October 27, 2012. Visited November 17, 2012.

Robley, A., D. Purdey, M. Johnston, M. Lindeman, F. Busana, and K. Long. 2007. Experimental Trials to Determine Effective Fence Designs for Feral Cat and Fox Exclusion. *Ecological Management & Restoration* 8:3(Dec):193-198.

Schmidt, P. M., R.R. Lopez, and B.A. Collier. 2007. Survival, Fecundity, and Movements of Free-Roaming Cats. *Journal of Wildlife Management* 71(3):915–919.

Vantassel, S. M. 2012. Wildlife Management Professionals Need to Redefine the Terms: Lethal Control, Nonlethal Control, and Live Trap. *Human-Wildlife Interactions* 6:2(Fall):335–338.

Chapter 6. **Trapping**

The feral cat lobby continues to claim that trapping and removal (i.e. euthanize or adopt) doesn't work. But how can they claim that trapping doesn't work when trapping is the means by which cats are obtained for Trap-Neuter-Return (TNR) programs? How is it more efficient to release/adopt cats than to simply euthanize?

I fully acknowledge that trapping is time intensive and efficiency can vary widely. One study had a capture rate of over 7 cats per 100 trap nights while another had a capture rate of 1.3 cats per 100 trap nights. While the latter figure is certainly low, cats were still captured. When people criticize the efficacy or efficiency of trapping, consider how applicable eradication programs on islands are for control of cats on the mainland. First, how experienced were the trappers? Did the program hire professional wildlife control operators or did the technicians have to learn on the job? Second, how many restrictions were imposed on the types of tools available? Third, how educated were the cats? Was this the first or fourth attempt at eradication? Finally, how available is food to the cats that would compete with the traps. It is hard to trap cats when food provided by a "feeder" is readily available.

Trapping cats will increasingly become a greater part of the animal damage control industry as cat populations continue to grow across the country. The threat cats pose to public health and wildlife populations demand that something be done. Until governments enact sensible legislation, cat control will be a potential landmine for your business. Don't forget to charge. Cat control is one job where charging by the day along with a bounty on the cats is totally appropriate. You can easily spend a great deal of time and money trapping cats. Make sure you don't. If you decide to perform cat control, don't cut any corners and adopt the highest ethics. Failure to follow these suggestions could destroy you.

## Ethics

Whenever you decide to trap, be sure to follow the highest ethical practices. Do more than what the law requires. It is best to check the traps as often as possible. At minimum, the traps should be checked every 24 hours. It is best to check the traps following the times when the cats are most active. Typically, this means you will check traps in the morning. But if feeding takes place during mid-day, checking traps at dusk may be preferable.

Those of you in business should consider employing electronic-monitoring systems that notify you as soon as the trap closes. Removing trapped cats quickly, not only reduces stress to the cats and thereby increase humaneness of the control method, but rapid removal helps reduce the likelihood that un-trapped cats will identify the traps as dangerous. Be familiar with the traps prior to their use. Make sure you know how to handle skunks prior to setting your first trap. Skunks have a terrible tendency to enter traps not set for them. Additionally, consider what is in 1 foot radius of the trap. Accidentally caught raccoons will destroy anything they can reach, much to the dismay of the trap setter and property owner.

### Types of Cat Problems

Cat problems can be divided into 2 categories, inside and outside jobs. Inside jobs are those where you are hired to remove cats from a building or structure, and are the easiest.

### Inside Jobs

Sometimes cats must be removed from inside buildings. It could be due to the owner's death, a stray entering, or whatever. Finding a cat in a building can be difficult if rooms are cluttered. Try to reduce the cat's ability to move. If you can locate the cat and get to it, you may just want to use a catch-pole (Fig. 1) or cat grasper to get it, place in a cage, and remove it. Always reduce its movement area (i.e. close doors etc.). Use caution when employing a catch-pole around a cat's neck. They have thin neck muscles and it is easy to injure or kill a cat by cinching down on the loop too hard and/or too long. It is preferable to have at least one leg through the loop so all the pressure is not on the neck.

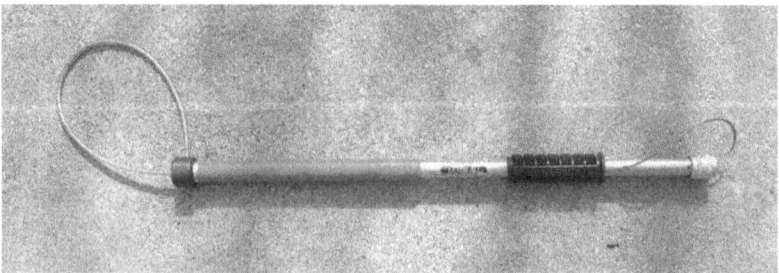

**Fig. 1.** *Catch-pole.*

If you can't find it or it is too difficult to get it, simply place traps inside the room. If the cat won't enter the cage trap then consider placing water inside the cage trap. If that doesn't work consider switching to another device, such as a padded-jaw foothold bedded in the kitty litter (see the foothold section below).

**Outside Jobs**

Outside jobs as the term suggests is where you need to reduce the present population of stray/feral cats. This job is by far the most difficult and dangerous. I would recommend taking the following steps. First, try to see if there is a non-trapping solution to the problem. Little things like securing sheds (after driving out the cat), removing food, fencing a garden etc. may solve or reduce the problem to a tolerable level. Second, (here my comments are directed to wildlife control operators but if trapping for yourself, be sure to follow the concerns too) if trapping must be utilized and is legal, require that the client guarantees in writing that the cats are not owned. Make the client confirm that the cat(s) that was/were caught are not owned. Make the client perfectly aware of the fact that if anything goes wrong, he is in hot water (i.e. liable) along with you. Carefully inquire whether any trapping has been done/tried prior to your arrival. Educated cats take forever to recapture. So you will need to charge accordingly. Finally, you will need to determine if the location you will be trapping welcomes cat trapping or is hostile to cat trapping. Don't simply assume that everyone at a business or apartment complex welcomes you.

**Types and Uses of Traps**

**Cage/Box Traps**

Cage/box traps are frequently and mistakenly called "live traps". While they do capture animals alive, people make the mistake that other traps (like footholds) kill. To reduce this confusion, I will refer to them as cage and box traps. Cage traps have wire-mesh walls. Box traps have solid walls (Fig. 2). Both function in similar ways by imprisoning the animal by envelopment. For the purposes of this section, the traps will be interchangeable. Just keep in mind that sometimes a box trap may be necessary to protect children and pets or used as a change-up in areas where cats have become educated to heavy trapping activity.

Cage/box traps also utilize different mechanisms for the doors. Gravity doors employ the force of gravity to close the door when

**Fig. 2.** *Cage trap (left) and box trap (right).*

the trigger fires. These traps typically are home-made or are using an older design. They have the advantage of allowing for easy release of the animal; simply roll the trap on its back and the door usually opens. This advantage is very helpful for when a skunk is captured.

In contrast, spring-loaded doors have a spring to close the door. These traps are a more recent design and are typically used by professionals. The spring-fired door allows the trap to close even when placed on sloped ground. The downside is that the trapper must manually open the door in order to permit the release of an animal.

Cage/box trap sizes can vary from 6 × 6 × 9.5 to 10 × 12 × 36 inches. Cats can be crowded into small traps, but traps must be long enough to fit the entire length of the body when triggered. Height is more important than width. Minimum height is 9 inches. All cage traps should be modified with at least 50% of the trap covered (Fig. 3). Covers can consist of cardboard, cloth, boards, or other solid objects that will provide protection for any animals trapped in the cage. This sheltered area is important to protect the trapped cat from stress from the sun, wind, rain, or snow. Covers can be adjusted depending on season and approaching weather conditions. Box

**Fig. 3.** *Wrap cardboard or other protective material on 3 sides (except the bottom) of the cage and wire it in place.*

traps will do this for you, but you need to be careful about their use during the hot summer months. My own research found that box traps can have internal temperatures several degrees higher than that experienced by cage traps. While this temperature increase is beneficial in winter months, it might be dangerous in the hot summer. As mentioned earlier, consider environmental conditions. Full sun exposure may be a great idea for traps placed in northern climates during the winter. But it may be a bad idea to do the same during the summer.

Box traps may provide an additional benefit by exploiting the cat's tendency to investigate enclosed spaces. For example, most pet cats will investigate empty cardboard boxes. They can also mimic a tipped over trash can. The downside of box traps is that they hold odors (e.g. urine and feces) that may frighten potential cats away.

### Location, Location, Location

The effectiveness of trapping is directly tied to the location of the traps. The principle is to place traps where the animals are rather than trying to lure the animals to where your traps are. Animals are just as lazy as humans. Don't force them to find your traps. That being said, you must also consider public perception. As a general rule, place traps out of public view whenever possible. What people don't see, they can't damage or interfere with. A great challenge with trapping comes from so-called "cat-lovers" who will release animals from your

**Fig. 4.** *Trap placed inside a plastic trash can.*

traps, thereby educating them. Educated cats are extremely hard to trap. All cage traps should be painted with flat (non-glossy) paint to help reduce shine. This is not so much for the cats as it is to reduce the visibility of the traps to people. Think creatively about how to hide your traps. Sometimes it is easier than you might think. For example, place trash cans on their side and place the trap inside (Fig. 4). You may also hide traps behind sheets of plywood (Figs. 5a,b). Other ways to hide traps include, placing them in bushes, burying them with leaves, or under porches or in garages. Use your creativity to think of other ways to hide them from nosey people.

A key advantage with out-of-sight trap placement is that the trapped animals will be more likely to be protected against the elements (sun, wind, rain, snow). Trapped animals can suffer stress, so consider their well-being and the environmental conditions they will be experiencing while they wait for you to arrive.

Sometimes the best site to trap cats is not the best because the landowner won't grant permission or the employees or others will molest your traps. In these circumstances, use Google Earth or a topographical map to identify alternative locations. Trapping on the interior areas of wooded areas or along edges of woods (par-

**Fig. 5a.** *Plywood hiding a 2-door trap.*

**Fig. 5b.** *Side-view of same trap. Note newspaper on the floor of the trap to prevent cats from stepping on the wire floor.*

ticularly stream beds) can be effective locations not only to hide traps but to capture cats. Sometimes contacting other landowners will give you access there. Because cats roam a ¼ of a mile or more from their denning sites, you should be able to locate alternative trapping areas.

All traps must be stable, so as not to wobble when a cat steps on the trap floor. Level the ground whenever possible. Use a shovel to scrape the soil level. If that isn't possible, traps may be stabilized by laying blocks (2 to 5 lbs) on top, by staking, or by wedging the trap between cinderblocks or a solid vertical object. Cover the floor of the cage traps with soil or newspaper as many feral cat websites state that cats don't like to walk on the wire. While trap stability is critical to effective trapping, don't place too much weight on the traps. Test-fire the stabilized trap to ensure it is functional. If all appears well, then reset.

As a general rule, cage traps can be effective and preferable in situations where cats have not been previously cage-trapped. Some contend that traps must be very clean and free of foreign odors, at least at the beginning of the control of a colony. As long as the traps are being used to control the same colony, they don't need to be cleaned after each capture. You will need to clean them if you are using them to trap in a new colony. Sometimes you may need to have a clean cage when attempting to capture a few lone males. Cage traps can be deodorized and cleaned by use of a weed burner (be careful of causing a fire), spray washing, or just leaving outdoors for the wind/rain to clean the trap. Understand that cleaning will reduce the lifespan of your traps, but it still may be necessary in order to catch wary cats. Do NOT use heat with plastic traps. Avoid using a power washer as the force of the water may splash back on you and enter an open mouth. Soak with cleaning solutions (e.g. Lysol®) and triple rinse and air dry.

If the cats are not educated, employ the following techniques.

1. Get an accurate number of the cats present. At minimum, you should have enough traps for the number of cats present. This is essential as you want to remove the cats quickly. But it is also important because cats avoid traps when they witness other cats in those traps.
2. Set the traps in discrete locations, whenever possible. Remember, out-of-sight is out of mind. Be discreet and ensure your contract states that you have the right to end the job if the traps are molested. Some trappers set their traps at night and pick them up before dawn. Obviously, you will be using cage or box traps. Use raccoon-size traps 10 × 12 × 32 inches but you can likely get away with traps 8 × 8 × 24 inch.
3. Pre-bait for several days to get the cats accustomed to the traps. Baits for cats would include, cat food both moist and dry. Dry is cheaper and doesn't rot. Keep your bait simple as you will need options when dealing with trap-wise cats. If you are using cage traps with treadle triggers to catch cats, simply place some of the bait on the treadle and the rest in the regular position. Since cats have a tendency to step next to what they eat you should have no problems catching them.
4. Set the traps and check on them every few hours for the reasons noted above. Sooner is better as you want to remove trapped cats

ASAP before other cats see the trapped cats and learn to avoid the cages. Cats can be very delicate when retrieving and consuming bait. A slender stepping stick in front of the trap pan can guide foot placement. Duct-taping a can of cat food to the treadle can help also. Avoid placing baits on stick or hooks as cats seem to prefer eating food on the ground rather than suspended. So if you do suspend food or lure, be sure some food is on the treadle or the trap floor. Some trappers may trap for a couple of nights to knock the population down, and then return in a week or so to remove the rest. The gap in time gives the colony the opportunity to calm down and adjust to a new normal.

## Attractants

I have chosen to use the term attractants because the term covers a broader array of items used to entice cats into or to a trap. Technically, baits refer to food-based attractants. Baits interest cats because they can be eaten. As such, they are usually solid. Lures, on the hand, are typically liquid or liquid-solid mix. While lures do encompass food odors, they also can be formulated to exploit cat interest based on territorial/sexual needs and curiosity. But cats can be attracted to traps through visual and audible cues. So while food-based baits/lures will comprise the bulk of your trapping work, keep in mind the other techniques mentioned as they may be needed when cats become accustomed to food-based baits. Having alternative attractants available can be necessary to capture a cat that has associated danger with the bait you were using previously.

Many theories exist regarding the use of attractants. Some believe that the bait should be "different" than what the cat normally feeds on. Others think it should be similar to what it is feeding on. Some think that cats in colder climates select for higher energy foods than those in colder climates. The key is to use what works in your area (keep records) and be open to change it up. The following attractants can be used in any combination. Experiment.

### Food-based attractants

Cats are attracted to fats. While stories abound about cats eating ice cream, the fact is the cat was more interested in the fat (i.e. cream) than the sugar. Common baits for cats include dry and moist cat food. Fish packed in oil is particularly aromatic and enticing to cats as well as other carnivores. Other fatty foods attractive to cats include bologna sausage, deli roast beef, fishmeal, and Kentucky Fried Chicken. The challenge with these meat-based baits is they rot. Cats like fresh food. So replace the bait regularly or purchase it from professional bait manufacturers who have added preservatives to extend the freshness of the bait.

One bait called the Mel Hershberger bait is reported to hold up well in heat as well as attract cats. It can be made from 1 can of jack mackerel, stir in enough honey to make a medium thick paste. Add 1/8 oz tincture of asafoetida and stir. Optional—add a tsp of beaver castor for a different appeal. A sprinkling of sodium benzoate powder preserves the bait longer. A bit of mild light fish oil can help prevent the bait from drying out.

### Gland-based Attractants

Many commercial brands of lures offered by professional trap supply dealers are effective. Bobcat Anal Gland Lure, Canine Call, and Pro's Choice all manufactured by Russ Carmen have been used successfully in cat trapping campaigns. Research, however, shows that these may not be as effective as other options. Nevertheless, variety or changing attractants can be helpful in enticing cats that have avoided other lures. Ironically, cat urine did not work well as an attractant.

### Curiosity Attractants

One pen study found that catnip and matatabi performed twice as well as other lure/bait combinations in terms of getting a cat's attention. The trouble, however, is the lures were not used in conjunction with traps.

### Visual Attractants

For long range hunting, cats rely on visual cues as part of their hunting behavior. Visual lures can be attached to picture wire swivels to allow them to spin in light wind. Just attach aluminum tags, aluminum strips of foil, pink flagging tape, flashing bicycle lights, toy windmills on sticks, dangling feathers (check laws on the use of feathers, Fig. 6.), CD or DVD disks, to name a few.

Regardless of the attractant used, it is critical that it be presented properly. Cats can't be captured by attractants they can't perceive. We have already discussed location. The second principle is to endeavor to place attractants at eye-level whenever possible. Keeping attractants off the ground helps make it easier for the cat to visualize the attractant but also to smell it, as the molecules are more

**Fig. 6.** *Visual attractant made of rabbit or similar fur and hung from a wire.*

exposed to the air. Paste baits can be hung from bait sticks made of 1-inch PVC pipe with T-end cap or a "Y" stick (Fig. 7.) that are suspended through the top of the cage at the back of the trap. The T-end cap or the "Y" prevent the stick from falling through the top of the cage. Note, never cut a hole in box traps as this will weaken the trap's structure. Hanging baits also helps reduce loss to ants.

When using attractants that won't adhere to the bait sticks, then place them inside a PVC pipe holder (Fig. 8). This device can hold mushy baits like moist cat food, sardines, etc. A 2-inch PVC pipe with one threaded and one non-threaded end caps, PVC adhesive, and an eye-bolt

**Fig. 7.** *Bait holders. PVC pipe (left) and "Y" stick (Right) for use with paste baits.*

**Fig. 8.** *PVC bait holder for moist baits.*

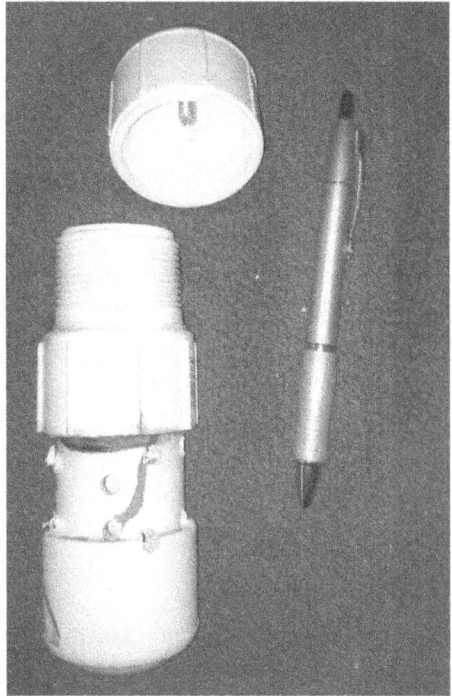

and screw, and a ¼-inch drill bit with drill are all that is needed. Drill air holes around the circumference of the pipe to let the air get at the bait. Don't put holes in the bottom as this will allow the bait to leak out. Simply place the bait inside, screw on the cap, and suspend with a wire in the rear of the trap. To clean, just place in 10% bleach solution.

## Blind Cage-Trapping

If you know that cats are using a particular hole, be it under a fence or in a building, you can use 2-door traps to make what is known as a blind set. Blind sets don't utilize attractants, thus are blind. Whatever comes through the opening must enter the trap. These sets are extremely effective (Fig. 9). Spring-loaded double doors are more forgiving than gravity door models. Be sure the trap doors are close enough to the vertical portion of the opening to prevent cats from refusing to enter the trap and climb over it. A cloth over the length of the trap helps give a tunnel appearance so the cat will "walk to the light." Side boards must be secure to keep

**Fig. 9.** *Two-door trap set at a hole under the fence.*

the cat directed to the opening. Test fire your trap before you leave to ensure the doors aren't so close to the wall that they jam. I suggest ensuring that baited traps be nearby to catch cats trying to enter the opening from the non-obstructed side.

### Additional Cage/Box Trapping Techniques

Non-target captures are one of the greatest challenges to trapping. When non-targets are captured, you lose the ability to trap the animal you wanted (the target animal) with that trap. You also lose time. Below are three sets useful for reducing the number of non-targets captured by your cage or box trap. They won't stop all non-target animals from entering your traps, but they will reduce captures of skunks and other animals that aren't good climbers.

## 1. Raised-set technique.

This set requires that you place the trap on a platform at least 19 inches off the ground (Fig. 10). Be sure the platform and the trap are secured with screws or wire so the whole set doesn't wobble and the trap doesn't fall off. The photo shows how you can make the cat jump 2 levels to get to the trap. The trap is stabilized. The trap is also covered to provide the cat shelter from the elements.

## 2. Chimney-tube Technique

This option was adapted from a trapping technique used with Conibears®. You construct a box of plywood that can set over the top of the cage-trap. The horizontal part needs to be as long as the trap plus 14 inches so that the chimney portion will provide the cat at least a 12-inch opening before it can enter the trap. Chimney height shouldn't be greater than 20 inches (Fig. 11). Be sure the trap and the box are stabilized. Neither should move when the cat steps on or into them.

**Fig. 10.** *Raised-set technique.*

**Fig. 11.** *Chimney-tube set.*

### 3. Flat-hole Technique
This box is identical to the chimney-tube except that it lacks the chimney extension (Figs. 12a,b).

### Trapping Trap Wise Cats

Here are some tips I gleaned from others. The tips are listed in order that you should try them.

Wire the door open, put food in the front for a couple of days or until cats begin to feed (which could take up to several weeks), then begin placing bait further into the cage until the cats get comfortable enough for you to set the trap. Understand that other animals may be taking the bait, such as opossums or raccoons, so use a trail camera or witnesses to verify the food is actually being taken by cats. Remove alternative food sources. Trail cameras may be quite helpful at this point to identify trap molesters, feeders, and smart cats. Consider change-ups to your sets. Tricks to try on educated cats would be changing bait. Try adding valerian root oil (*Valeriana officinalis*), catnip (*Nepeta cataria*), silver vine (*Actinidia polygama* and *Actinidia kolomikta*), Snowball Tree or Guelder Rose (*Viburnum opulus*). Note that kittens under 8 weeks of age tend to not like cat-

**Fig. 12a,b.** *Flat-hole Technique*

nip and Siamese cats can be indifferent. Feathers, or even rolled up aluminum foil, can catch cats' attention and exploit their curiosity

Try larger traps. Sometimes cats feel crowded. You should also consider changing traps. New traps have been developed, such as the clam trap and gravity traps. Using a different kind of trap gives the cat a new look and will likely reduce refusal rates.

Use a double-door trap, or clam traps.

Try a trap that doesn't look like a trap ... like a solid walled Durapoly.

Remove odors by rinsing traps, placing them outdoors for several weeks, or flaming them with a propane torch (metal traps only when flaming). When rinsing traps, consider where the water and back splash may go as you could expose yourself or others to infectious agents (this is particularly true when cleaning box traps). If exposing traps to weather, select locations where soil will not be disturbed or gardens planted. When flaming cage traps, consider fire safety. Heat the metal but not so much to turn it red.

Try using a drop trap which consist of a cage that is leaned on one end with a stick that is attached to a rope. Bait is placed on the ground or a solid base, when the cat(s) is/are feeding inside, you pull the string and drop the cage. Several videos are available on YouTube that demonstrate the process.

## Tools of Last Resort

The following traps should only be used if they are legal, the situation requires rapid removal of cats, and the land restricts public access. I cannot emphasize this enough. These traps are very controversial. If you are not familiar with their proper use don't use them.

## Footholds

Despite the way footholds are demonized by the animal rights protest industry, footholds can play a vital role in removing cats from a location. Their utility, low cost, and humaneness make them a valuable tool in your cat control arsenal. A key problem with footholds is the risk of injury to captured animals. While animals can and are injured in cage traps, the injuries in cages are usually self-inflicted so are less important in the view of the public. The #1 Victor Soft Catch® and the #3 Victor Soft Catch® have both been successfully used in the control of cats on islands (Fig. 13) but the 1.5 should be more than enough for most situations. The traps' short chains, shock spring, and rubberized jaws reduce leg damage. The short chain prevents the cat from gaining too much speed as it tries to strain against the trap. The padded jaw increases the surface area (thereby reducing pressure) as well as softens the initial blow upon closing. You can also use #1.5 padded-jaw traps. Injury can be further reduced by using a remote trap monitoring system capable of notifying the trapper when a capture is made.

As a general rule, footholds are needed when cats become wise to cage/box traps or when the area is too large or remote to permit the use of cage traps. One research paper suggests that footholds are the most effective tool for use in landscapes smaller than 1200 hectares.

## Setting footholds

Place the traps in a shallow hole the size and shape of the set trap. Cover the pan with waxed paper and then cover the trap with sifted soil, sawdust, or potting soil. Place the bait material 2 to 4 inches beyond the trap that the cat must step on the trap to reach

**Fig. 13.** *#1.5 Padded jaw foothold with 4-coils, shock-spring, and in-line swivels. When trapping cats, remove 2 of the coils.*

it). Traps can be set at entrances to holes where cats are hiding, entryways to buildings, in kitty litter boxes, or near garbage cans.

The trigger of the trap, also called the pan, should be 2 to 4 inches from the bait and offset from the bait, which may be placed inside something as simple as a hole. Employ a backing to prevent the cats from approaching the bait from the wrong side. Consult coyote trapping books for more details on the use of footholds to capture cats. It doesn't matter which side you offset the trap, either left or right because research shows cats as population favor right or left foot about equally so your odds are 50/50.

To release a cat from a foothold, first, use a catch-pole (with a locking mechanism) or have a partner cover the cat with a blanket (hold it firmly). Second, stretch the cat away from the trap. If alone, place your foot on the pole to free your hands to grab the trap. Depress the springs to loosen the jaws. Once the cat realizes the pressure is gone, it will immediately pull out its leg. Wear gloves and other protective equipment. Place cat inside a cage/box trap for transport to its final destination. When using a catch-pole be careful when securing it around the cat's neck. Cats lack strong neck muscles, so cinching down the cable can cause severe damage. It is better to have the loop behind at least one leg so that the loop is around the chest to reduce the risk of damage to the cat's neck.

## Conibear-Style Traps

Conibear-style traps are the only traps-designed to kill that are mentioned in this book. I use the term conibear-style because Conibear® is actually a trade name, but in common parlance they mean the same thing. So when you purchase the traps, call them Conibears®. I am not going to detail their use. If you are interested in learning more about them consult the literature at the end of this chapter. The New Zealanders have the best information on using conibear-style traps. However, their research appears to have been with a trap similar in size to the No. 110 conibear-style trap, except with a stronger spring. Since that trap has only one spring and it is no longer manufactured, I suggest using a No. 120 conibear-style trap with a 4½ × 4½ jaw spread. This trap has 2 springs rather than just one, which should improve its killing power. Select conibear-style traps with jaws that close completely flush. As with cage traps, conibear-style traps can be used in baited or blind sets.

A word of caution: if I told you to be careful with trapping cats you must be triply cautious when trapping cats with Conibears®. Mistaken captures can't be undone. Conibear-style traps must be used with the greatest of care. Furthermore, though the conibear-style traps are kill traps, they rarely kill instantaneously. As of this writing, no kill trap has been successful in killing cats instantly (or even within 3 minutes) 100% of the time. It is doubtful that such a trap could be made, but we can certainly hope. Conibear-style traps should be used as a last-last resort and then only by individuals experienced with their use and where legal.

## Resources

Caras, R. A. 1989. *A Cat is Watching: A Look at the Way Cats See Us.* NY: Simon and Schuster.

Clapperton, B. K., C. T. Eason, R. J. Weston, A. D. Woolhouse, and D. R. Morgan. 1994. Development and Testing of Attractants for Feral Cats, *Felis catus* L. *Wildlife Research* 21:388-399.

Corrigan, R. 2005. Rodent Control. *Pest Control Technology* (May):59-62, 80.

Feral cats—Impact and control. Wildlife Research and Management Pty Ltd. No date. http://www.wildliferesearchmanagement.com.au/Fact%20sheet_feral%20cats.pdf ; visited Sept 9, 2012.

Feral Cat Message Boards, visited fall of 2012.

Fitzwater, W. D. Feral Cats, In: *Prevention and Control of Wildlife*

*Damage.* Editors, Scott E. Hygnstrom, Robert M. Timm, Gary E. Larson. 1994. University of Nebraska-Lincoln. 2 vols.

Hanson, C. C., J. E. Bonham, K. J. Campbell, B. S. Keitt, A. E. Little, and G. Smith. 2010. The Removal of Feral Cats from San Nicolas Island: Methodology. *Proc. Vertbr. Pest Conf.* 24:72-78.

Marchewka, M. 2012. Fur Taker Talk: Tricks, Tips, and Musings. *Fur Taker Magazine* 48:11(Nov):28-9.

Marks, B. K. and R. S. Duncan. 2009. Use of Forest Edges by Free-Ranging Cats and Dogs in an Urban Forest Fragment. *Southeastern Naturalist* 8(3):427-436.

Molsher, R. L. Trapping and demographics of feral cats (*Felis catus*) in central New South Wales. *Wildlife Research,* 2001, 28, 631–636

Nogales, M., A. Martin, B. R. Tershy, C. J. Donlan, D. Veitch, N. Puerta, B. Wood, and J. Alonso. 2004. A Review of Feral Cat Eradication on Islands. *Conservation Biology,* 18:2(April):310-319.

Recio, M. R., R. Mathieu, R. Maloney, and P. J. Seddon. 2010. First Results of Feral Cats (*Felis catus*) Monitored with GPS Collars in New Zealand. *New Zealand Journal of Ecology* 34(3):288-296.

Risbey, D. A., M. Calver, and J. Short. 1997. Control of Feral Cats for Nature Conservation. I. Field Tests of Four Baiting Methods. *Wildlife Research* 24:319-326.

Robertson, S. A. 2007. Review Article: A Review of Feral Cat Control. *Journal of Feline Medicine and Surgery* 10:366-375.

Schmidt, P. M., R. R. Lopez, and B. A. Collier. 2007. Survival, Fecundity, and Movements of Free-Roaming Cats. *Journal of Wildlife Management* 71(3):915–919.

Sharp, T. and G. Saunders. 2005. *CAT002 Trapping of feral cats use cage traps.* Natural Heritage Trust: NSW Department of Primary Industries. Australia. 10pp.

Strauss, B., editor. 2011. Animals Have a Favorite Hand. *Science Illustrated* 4:5(Sept/Oct):50-55.

Vantassel, S. M. 2012. Wildlife Management Professionals Need to Redefine the Terms: Lethal Control, Nonlethal Control, and Live Trap. *Human-Wildlife Interactions* 6:2(Fall):335–338.

Warburton, B. and N. Poutu. 2002. Effectiveness of three trapping systems for killing feral cats. DOC SCIENCE INTERNAL SERIES 50. Department of Conservation P.O. Box 10-420 Wellington, New Zealand http://www.doc.govt.nz/documents/science-and-technical/DSIS50.pdf

Chapter 7. **Shooting**

Shooting cats can be an effective management tool in controlling cats. Again as noted with the chapter on trapping above, make sure you **FOLLOW THE LAW.** You will have two legal issues confronting you. The first relates to shooting no matter what the target is. Most areas of the U.S. restrict the discharge of firearms (yes air-powered rifles are considered firearms) within 300 feet of a structure or right-of-way unless appropriate permissions are obtained. Towns and municipalities may prohibit the discharge of firearms within their limits regardless. Bottom line, **KNOW THE LAW.**

The second issue is the controversy of shooting cats or in any way harming them. I have warned you about this topic repeatedly. Don't forget, even if it is legal or not prohibited to shoot cats, that doesn't mean you won't get in trouble if someone complains. Being legal does not mean you won't be vilified in the public and face a mountain of legal bills. Animal rights protest industry advocates are looking for ways to prosecute people who kill any animal, let alone an animal as popular as cats. You have been warned.

### Ethics

If you decide that shooting is an option for you, take the time to understand your weapon. Learn how to safely use it, clean it, and accurately shoot it. Firearm ballistics is a huge and complicated field. You don't have to know everything but you should have a good idea concerning effective range, windage, bullet drop, etc. The following site can be helpful in describing issues with the .22LR: http://www.gunsmoke.com/guns/1022/22ballistics.html. The information can be useful in thinking about the kind of concerns you should have with other firearms.

You must also make safety of paramount importance. Know what you are shooting and consider down-range range risks. Always remember that once the gun is fired, you cannot retrieve the bullet.

A good rule of thumb is to be able shoot a quarter-sized grouping (at least 90% of the time) at the average distance to the target your ground conditions will allow and within the gun's effective killing range. Accuracy is even more important when using air-rifles, which may lack the knock-down power of traditional firearms. Shotguns allow for more flexibility but you still need to be familiar with

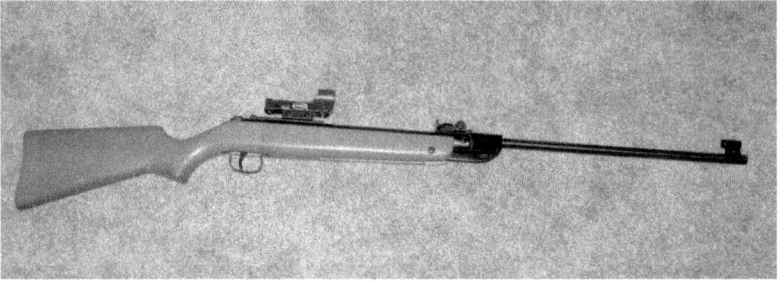

**Fig. 1.** *Break-style air-rifle with dot scope.*

shot patterns, choke settings, and barrel lengths. You don't want to wound animals; you want clean kills that are performed safely. Always sight-in your gun before shooting to ensure its accuracy.

## Equipment

It should be obvious that there isn't a lot of published research on the proper hunting of cats. To help expand the information here, I have used a woodchuck (*Marmota monax*) as proxy for cats. If the gun can kill a woodchuck then it will likely kill a cat. Nevertheless, hunters have used .22, .222, and 12-gauge shotguns with #6 shot (or lower) to shoot cats. The technological improvements made with pellet rifles also make these guns worth considering (Fig. 1). One specialist recommended that shooters choose .22 caliber air rifles that can provide pellet velocities of at least 950 feet per second. She also suggested avoiding the use of flathead pellets. Flatheads are only for target practice. Instead use pointed, ballistic, or hollow point lead pellets. Practice with each of these pellets to get a sense of their respective penetration ability. Ideally, the pellet or bullet should not pass through the cat. You want all the energy to dissipate inside the cat. This also makes shooting safer as the pellet or bullet isn't going to hit something you didn't target.

I haven't mentioned archery. I don't doubt its efficacy, particularly in regards to the usability of crossbows. However, I didn't find any publications that mentioned their use with cats or similar-sized animals. Archery is certainly safer and quieter than using firearms. The downside is that the public may be even more incensed by shooting cats with a bow than with a gun. Additionally, some states still prohibit the use of crossbows. So, as always, consider local and state laws BEFORE doing anything.

### Optional but useful equipment

Eye and ear protection is strongly advised.

Scopes are recommended. Night scopes allow for great versatility. Consult state and local laws about hunting, shooting, regulations, especially those that concern shooting at night. Bi-pods are quite helpful in improving gun stability and ultimately accuracy.

### Safety

ALWAYS, CONSIDER DOWN-RANGE AND RICOCHET RISKS BEFORE SHOOTING. Never forget that what goes up must come down and once the projectile leaves you don't have a redo button. Consider that .22 caliber rifles are dangerous to more than a mile. Shotguns can pose risks out to a few hundred yards and have a reported maximum range of almost 600 yards. Pellet rifles are dangerous out to 750 yards (Fig. 2). Use the right firearm, ammunition, projectile, etc., for the situation you are facing. Don't use the shooting equivalent of a sledgehammer when a regular hammer will do. More power means more down-range risk. However, don't use so little power that you risk not killing the cat efficiently or humanely.

**Fig. 2.** *This window shows the effects of a projectile on a window.*

**Hunting Technique**

Hunting falls into 2 categories: opportunistic and planned. Opportunistic refers to situations where you were not hunting cats *per se*, but would take advantage of the "opportunity" should it arise. This type of hunting is only practical when you know the area well enough that shooting can be performed safely.

Planned hunting refers to your actually scheduling a hunt. Before you ever begin to hunt, survey the area with a topographical map and/or Google Earth map. Discuss with the landowner where the cats are seen most frequently. You will need to know where you can shoot safely before you begin. Scouting should not be short-changed. When hunting, pay careful attention to the birds and squirrels as they will announce when the cat is nearby.

Consider noise. Choose sub-sonic rounds whenever possible. You don't want the "crack" of your firearm to draw unnecessary attention to yourself. For the shotgun, try the metro-barrel (Fig. 3). It is an extra-long barrel that when used with sub-sonic rounds significantly reduces the report of the gun.

Here are a few suggestions that may help improve your hunting success.
- Bait. If feeding has been done, have the feeding continue or move it to a location where shooting would be safe. Consult relevant laws about shooting over bait. It is best to have bait areas spread out so that shooting a cat in one station will be less likely to disturb a cat feeding at another.
- Predator calls. One author suggests using predator calls, such as electronic calls. Mouse squeakers or rabbit distress may be effective.
- Get off the ground. Shooting from an elevated spot can be quite advantageous as well as dangerous. Lots of hunters have been severely injured and some killed falling from stands. Learn how to use stands correctly before you get off the ground.
- Shoot from a blind. Cats have excellent vision and hearing. Don't let them associate you with danger. Shooting from a familiar object such as a vehicle can be quite helpful. Check state laws regarding shooting from a motor vehicle.
- Use visual distractions. Suspended decoys of fur or feathers can help fixate a cat's attention giving you time to shoot.
- Use hunting dogs. Dogs can be helpful in finding and treeing cats.
- Hunt at night. Night-vision technology, though pricey, provides an incredible advantage.

**Fig. 3.** *A shotgun with a metro-barrel (gun on right) in comparison with other firearms.*

Shooting involves significant safety risks and is heavily regulated by states, wildlife agencies, and municipalities. Consult all relevant authorities before using this technique and be sure the control of cats, including by shooting, is legal before initiating control.

**Shot Placement**

Information on shooting cats is scarce. The following information represents the best information I could find. Just a reminder, shooting cats will be staunchly opposed by people. It may also be considered cruel in your area. Be sure you are within the bounds of the law before you begin.

You have two general locations to place your shot: the head and the chest. Head shots present the most difficult location because the head may move after you pull the trigger. On the other hand, a well-placed shot may result in the cat's instant death, an event sometimes called "distant euthanasia." The goal of a head shot is to destroy as much brain material as possible. The images help show suggested placement. Figures 4 and 5 show where the bullet should travel when the cat is facing you. Figure 7 shows shot placement when the cat's head is in the profile position. You want to place the bullet between the eye and the ear along the imaginary line between the base of the ear and the corner of the eye. When shooting

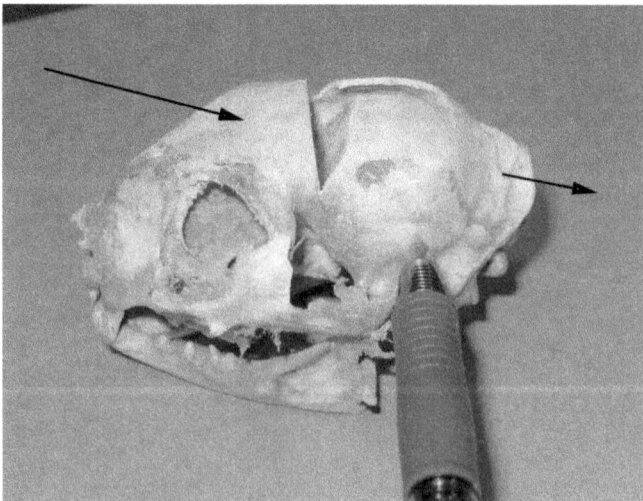

**Fig. 4.** *Lines show preferred trajectory for shooting a cat through the forehead.*

at the chest, the goal is to hit the heart and/or lungs. The heart, of course, is the preferred target as death will result more quickly than a lung shot. Note how these vital organs are in the area behind the front leg/shoulder on the lower third of the cat's body (Fig 6.)

Figure 7 tries to put all potential targets together in one image.

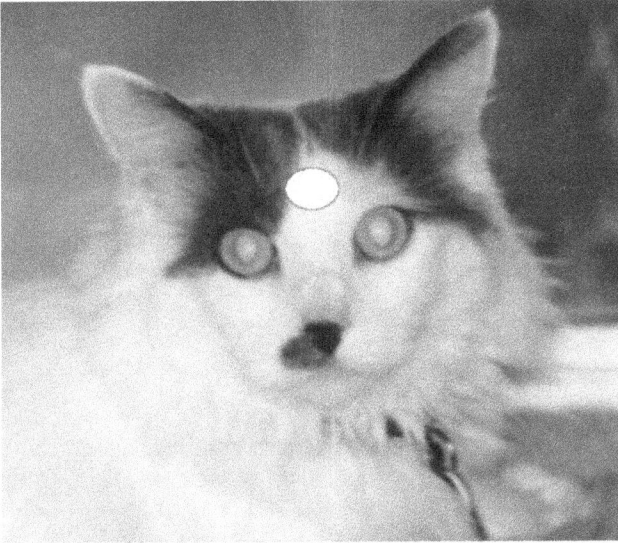

**Fig. 5.** *Target area for shooting a cat facing you.*

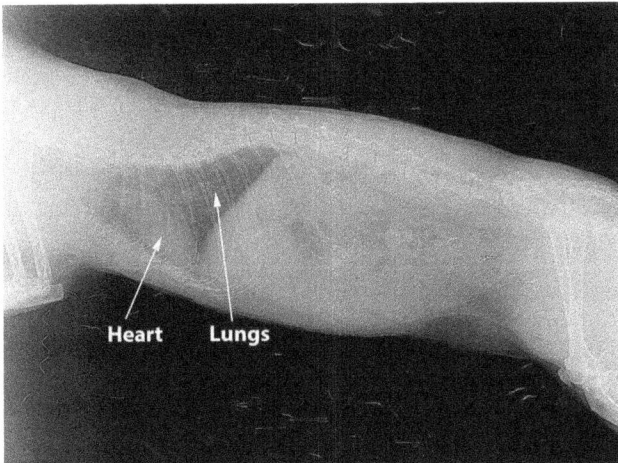

**Fig. 6.** *Relative position of the heart and lung in a cat. Adapted from an image from Shutterstock.*

**Fig. 7.** *Adapted from an image from Shutterstock.*

## Expectations

Hunting can play an important role in eliminating a cat population. However, it is time-intensive. Don't just consider the amount of time spent hunting. You have to include the time needed to become proficient with your firearm. You also must sight-in your gun before using it. It is probably best used in situations where the cats have gotten trap wise and stealthy to other control methods.

## Resources

Hanson, C. C., J. E. Bonham, K. J. Campbell, B. S. Keitt, A. E. Little, and G. Smith. 2010. The Removal of Feral Cats from San Nicolas Island: Methodology. *Proc. Vertbr. Pest Conf.* 24:72-78.

Kirkpatrick, R. D. and M. J. Rauzon. 1986. Foods of Feral Cats *Felis catus* on Jarvis and Howland Islands, Central Pacific Ocean. *Biotropica*, 18:1(Mar):72-75.

Nogales, M., A. Martin, B. R. Tershy, C. J. Donlan, D. Veitch, N. Puerta, B. Wood, and J. Alonso. 2004. A Review of Feral Cat Eradication on Islands. *Conservation Biology.* 18:2(April):310-319.

Sharp, T. and G. Saunders. 2005. *CAT002 Trapping of feral cats use cage traps.* Natural Heritage Trust: NSW Department of Primary Industries. Australia. 10pp.

Yahoo Answers. 2012. What is the Range of a 12-gauge Shotgun? Visited Oct. 28, 2012.

Chapter 8. **Techniques to Avoid**

Desperate people often resort to desperate measures. So I wanted to briefly mention several techniques that should be avoided. Readers should understand my opposition to these techniques is based on their usefulness of their role in the United States at the present time. Whether or not these techniques might be appropriate in other nations and contexts is an open question. Perhaps advances in technology will allow some of these techniques to be appropriate in the U.S. But for the moment, I think U.S. readers should avoid them. Readers in other countries need to consider my concerns carefully in the context of the legal and cultural environment in their area before using these techniques.

**Snares and Cable-restraints**

Snares and cable-restraints are suspended-loops that are placed in trails cables designed to capture the animal around the neck (Fig. 1). Snares are designed to kill and cable-restraints are designed to

**Fig. 1.** *This snare set actually was designed for coyote. But it is useful for illustration.*

hold but not kill the animal. I don't recommend these traps because of the expertise required, risk to non-targets, and the likelihood of killing the cat. Unlike dogs, cats will likely fight cable restraints, defeating their non-lethal use. Their weak necks make them vulnerable to asphyxiation even when the trapper doesn't intend to kill the cat. I strongly suggest these two methods be avoided until the technology improves.

## Toxicants

No toxicants or fumigants are registered by the Environmental Protection Agency for the control of house cats in the United States. It is illegal to use products in a manner not allowed on the label. As I stated at the beginning of the book, "Don't break the law." Use of toxicants is illegal in the U.S. So don't use them. The same rule applies for any so called "home-made" remedies.

# Chapter 9. Handling, Euthanizing, and Disposing of Cats

## Handling

**Direct Capture.** Direct capture refers to the action of obtaining control over a cat without the use of traps. Direct capture is useful in situations where the cat can be removed immediately such as when it is in a room or secure area. Tools to grab the cat include using a catch-pole (also known as a snare-pole), cat grasper, or by the use of gloved hands (I do not recommend this last method).

Catch-poles allow for greater control over the cat but if not used properly can result in the cat's death. Ideally, you should slip the loop over the head and one or both front legs before cinching down. When you finally get the cat's head in the noose draw it closed as fast as possible and then watch out. Ideally the noose should be around the cat's body, but this isn't always possible. Once snared, cats get very aggressive and extend their claws. I would caution you against getting scratched because of the dangers of cat-scratch fever. I am told it's like mononucleosis in the way it saps your energy. I also found that the cats don't leave their position easily either. You may have to pull rather hard to get them off the ground or out from under a bed or couch. If you need the animal to be more passive, and the noose is around its neck, keep the noose tight. The cat will eventually quiet down. You may even see the eyes seem to fog over. The cat isn't dead, only passed out. Don't keep the cat in this state any longer than necessary or it will die. This information isn't pretty. It is sometimes the grim reality. Fortunately, once you get experience with your equipment you should never need to use such drastic steps. It is far better to place the snare-pole loop over the body or at least behind one leg. Cinching a noose down around the neck of cat is not recommended as it can quickly lead to the death of the cat. Cat graspers would be better choice, provided you are comfortable with their use. A hand-net is a great choice but often not practical as cats crawl into areas where a net won't reach.

Whatever you do, be careful. Cats may not bite but they can scratch. If you are ever bitten go to the emergency room immediately. A cat's saliva is full is harmful bacteria which their sharp teeth will send deep into your tissues. These puncture wounds will need to be washed out by a professional, and you will need to be placed on antibiotics.

## Disposition & Disposal

### Relocation
Relocation is the movement and release of an animal within its home range. In layman's terms, if you capture a cat in someone's basement and release it in the backyard, that is relocation. I don't recommend relocation with unowned cats. Relocation is only legitimate, in my opinion, when used with an owned cat, such as in a rescue situation.

### Translocation
Translocation is what most people really mean when they say they want a cat relocated. Translocation is the movement and release of an animal outside/beyond its home range. Translocation is often perceived by people as being humane and effective. It allows the cat to continue to live its life but not be near enough to the homeowner to continue to be a problem. While translocation looks compassionate, looks can be deceiving. First, translocation simply moves the wildlife-killing cat to a new location to continue its ravaging ways. Second, the translocated cat must reorient itself to a new environment. Depending on the time of year of the release, the cat may have to find food, water, and shelter during winter conditions. Research on other species has found that translocated animals have lower life-expectancies than non-translocated animals. So while translocation may appear humane, the facts suggest otherwise. Finally, translocation increases the likelihood of disease transmission. A cat can be infected with a disease while appearing healthy. Transporting that cat to a new location simply helps the disease to spread to areas where the disease is not present, thereby putting animals in that location at risk.

In my opinion, the only places where cats should be translocated to are to their owners, an animal shelter, or to the grave (if the latter action is legal in your area).

## Capture Methods vs. Humane Killing vs. Euthanasia

It is important to distinguish between capture methods, humane killing, and euthanasia. For example, shooting an animal in the field is a capture method, not a euthanasia technique. The bullet may kill the animal but its primary function is to capture the target animal. For this reason, some experts add an additional category of humane-killing to distinguish euthanasia methods from other methods. To be clear, euthanasia only refers to the deliberate death of an animal that is killed under the direct control of a person, either instantly or while unconscious in a painless manner.

The emotional involvement people have with animals requires a recommendation that all killing of animals, whether by a capture device or by euthanasia methods, occurs out of public view. Failure to follow this advice may result in a great deal of unwanted attention and public scrutiny regarding your activities.

Readers should be reminded that killing cats involves legal risk at worst and damage to your reputation at best. Before you consider killing a cat you need to be sure that you have the legal right to do so.

Cats you should be especially cautious about killing:

- Ear tipped. Cats with a ¼-inch removed from the right ear have been ear-tipped. Ear-tipping is a method of identifying treated cats in the free-range cat lobby groups.

- Cats with collars.

- Cats that are micro-chipped.

- Cats that are spayed or neutered.

There may be other criterion that you should consider as well. In short, think long and hard before you decide to euthanize a cat. Euthanization is not reversible.

If you think you don't care, do a quick Google search using key words criminal charges and house cats. You may find a reference to "Md. man sentenced for shooting caged feral cat; 24-year-old sentenced to six months in Md.; man sentenced for shooting caged feral cat" by Edward Marshal of *Journal News* in Maryland ( http://www.journal-news.net ). This April 20, 2012 article tells of a man who shot a feral cat while it was in a cage trap. Even though the cat you are killing is not owned, remember that cats are considered domestic animals in many areas and cruelty rules apply.

Regardless of which method is used, endeavor to reduce stress to the animal as much as possible.

## Euthanasia

Euthanasia means good death ("eu" = good; "thanasia" = death), and it refers to techniques that are used to kill an animal as painlessly as possible. In general, to be considered euthanasia, death must occur instantaneously or while the animal is uncon-scious. Euthanasia, as it pertains to wildlife control, is defined as use of lethal methods that are safe for the WCO, the client, and the public, and are promptly carried out in a manner that causes the least amount of stress to the euthanized animal.

The American Veterinary Medical Association (AVMA) is one organization that determines whether a method meets the standard of euthanasia. Though a method may meet the AVMA standard of euthanasia, don't assume that others will agree. Gas chambers using carbon-monoxide are being decried as cruel by animal rightists/ animal protectionists. The hysterics of their language can be rather severe and beyond all evidence to the contrary. Some animal protectionists believe killing healthy cats no matter how it is done constitutes cruelty. But remember that euthanasia only refers to the killing of an animal in a painless manner, not whether the killing was justified. This chapter will only deal with methods that should meet the euthanasia criterion, not whether everyone will agree with the killing of cats.

**Euthanasia Techniques**

**Gas Chambers.**

Gas chambers are very controversial. The American Humane Association contends that cats should not be killed via chambers (http://www.americanhumane.org/). Unfortunately, this attitude has been successful in convincing a growing number of states to ban the practice. Check the rules in your state and municipality.

Carbon dioxide ($CO_2$) is the gas used to euthanize the animal. At the present time, many in the wildlife control industry consider euthanasia by carbon dioxide ($CO_2$) induced narcosis to be the most user-friendly of the AVMA 2007 euthanasia suggested methods. Bottled $CO_2$ gas is the method commonly used for euthanasia of animals in laboratory research settings. The method requires a chamber in which $CO_2$ replaces the available oxygen. The opportunity to euthanize an animal without injection, handling, or transfer is an advantage of $CO_2$. Carbon dioxide is readily available at welding supply centers, is relatively safe for humans to use, and will suppress the ability of an animal to experience pain prior to death.

A euthanasia chamber (Figure 1) is essential for euthanasia by $CO_2$. A chamber is simple to construct or you can purchase one from various providers. Chambers should be top-loading and large enough to hold your largest cage.

**Figure 1.** *A cage trap enclosed in a carbon-dioxide euthanasia chamber constructed with Plexiglas®.*

They can be as simple as a wooden box or a plastic trash can or barrel. If building a wooden box, seal the bottom and sides with glue and/or caulk so that they are air tight. The lid, however, should NOT be air tight. Drill a hole for the $CO_2$ delivery tube in the side of the box 1-inch from the bottom. Carbon dioxide is heavier than air. As the gas enters the chamber, the $CO_2$ displaces the air out the top of the box, which is why the lid should not be air tight.

A welding supply company or bottled gas supplier will be able to provide you with the $CO_2$ tank, gas regulator, flow meters, and tubing. Only use bottled $CO_2$ gas. Ask the supplier about all relevant laws and regulations concerning the handling, storage, and transportation of pressurized tanks. Improper handling of tanks can result in serious injuries and property damage.

Your goal is to minimize the stress of animals whenever possible. The following are suggestions for stress reduction:

1. Only one animal should be placed in a chamber at a time.
2. Animals should not see other animals being euthanized.
3. Animals should be handled as gently and as little as possible before and during the euthanasia process.

Animals can be kept calm by covering traps with old blankets or tarps. Speak in calm tones.

Fill the chamber with $CO_2$ at a rate of 20% per minute after a caged animal is placed in the chamber. The flow rate can be calculated for your particular chamber by following a procedure.

1. Measure the internal length, width, and height of the chamber in inches.
2. Multiply those 3 numbers (length × height × width) to determine the chamber's volume in cubic inches (e.g., 13 × 13 × 33-inch chamber = 5577 cubic inches).
3. Divide by 61 to convert the volume to liters (5577 divided by 61 = 91.4 liters).
4. Multiply 91.4 by 0.2 to obtain a fill rate of 20% per minute.
5. The result is 18.3 liters. Set the gravity-flow meter to a little more than 18 liters per minute and leave it on to fill the tank completely in 5 minutes.

After the chamber has filled, reduce the rate of flow to 3 to 5 liters per minute to save gas. Do not turn the flow off, so that the pressure remains positive and prevents fresh air from reentering the chamber. Expect the cat to tremble and audibly cry out.

One reference said dry-ice could be used to remove cats in holes or culverts. You will need about ½-pound per cubic yard (0.3 kg/m$^3$) of space. Animals succumbing to $CO_2$ frequently will start shaking their heads (it is believed that the $CO_2$ mixes with the moisture in the nasal passages creating a burning sensation from the carbonic acid), then exhibit shivering along with rapid and deep breathing, followed by lying down with shallow to barely perceptible breathing. Such sights can be disturbing. It is imperative that the death of the animal be confirmed.

### Shooting

When shooting is used as a means of euthanasia, personnel should be trained in the safe use of firearms and anatomy of the species involved. The firearm and ammunition should be appropriate for the size of the animal. For the cat, a .22 caliber short should be sufficient. You want the muzzle of the firearm with 1 to 2 inches of the target to reduce missing the target. Wait for the cat to stop moving its head.

The shot should be placed to destroy the maximum amount of brain matter. Consult the section in shooting for details on bullet placement. Although a correct shot will instantly render the animal

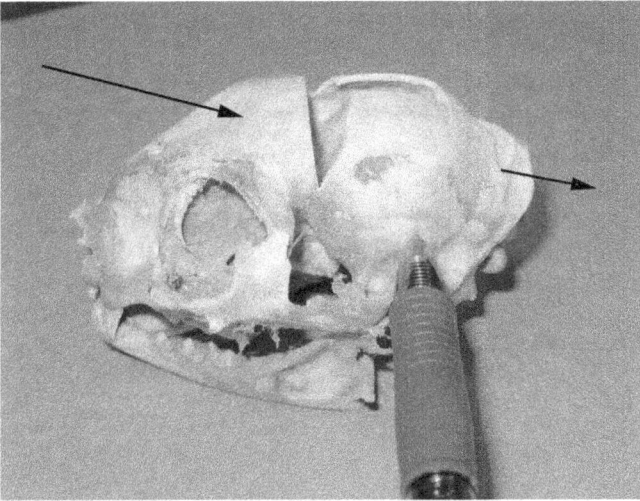

**Figure 2.** *Diagram illustrating bullet placement for euthanasia by shooting through the forehead.*

unconscious, thrashing, muscle spasms, and bleeding may continue afterwards for a brief amount of time. Note that shooting is not recognized as an appropriate technique by the AVMA.

Never shoot a cat in the head if the cat is under suspicion of rabies or if there is a potential of rabies exposure. Shooting in the brain will render testing invalid.

**Confirmation of Death**

Confirmation of death can be difficult in field settings. We recommend that you consider all the signs in the following discussion before determining whether the animal truly is deceased.

1. Respiration has stopped — check if the chest has stopped expanding and contracting for at least 3 minutes. You may have to look carefully, as some animals have very shallow breathing.

2. Corneal reflex has ceased — the animal should no longer blink (even when touched), the eyes should be fixed, and the pupils (the black portion of the eye) dilated. Eyes should be fixed and appear glazed.

3. Muscle tone is limp — dead animals will no longer be able to stand and should appear limp and flaccid.

4. Heart has stopped beating — a stethoscope and training is needed to properly identify this sign. Mucous membranes (e.g. gumline around teeth) should be pale/gray, not pink. When blanched, the pink color should not return. Always wear protective impermeable gloves if performing this test.

To make absolutely sure the animal is dead you may perform cervical dislocation on small animals or thoracic compression on large ones. Protect yourself from exposure to teeth and body fluids while performing these additional techniques. Rigor mortis (animal is stiff), putrification, decapitation, or loss of vital organs also are conclusive proof of death. Some states require that WCOs record the disposition of wildlife. Always keep accurate records.

## Disposal of Carcasses

Disposal of carcasses must be done safely, in a manner respectful of public sensitivities, and in accordance with state and local guidelines. Carcass disposal methods include:

1. Aboveground,
2. Belowground,
3. Incineration,
4. Disposal in a licensed landfill, and
5. Disposal with a dead animal dealer.

Always wear thick leather gloves to reduce the risk of being scratched or exposed to animal fluids when handling carcasses. Welder's gloves are durable and provide protection to the hands and the wrist. For additional protection, wear latex or vinyl gloves inside the leather gloves. Ticks and fleas present a health risk as they leave the dead carcass in search of a new host.

### Aboveground

Aboveground disposal is easy because no digging is involved. It is gaining in popularity as an environmentally responsible way to recycle carcasses back into the ecosystem. Unfortunately, aboveground disposal increases the likelihood of attracting scavengers that feed on carcasses. This method also raises the strong possibility that the carcasses will be discovered. Dogs may bring carcasses back to their owners and hikers or hunters may stumble upon them. Either of these events will likely result in a full-on investigation by the authorities. So use this method only when you have strong control of the location, if at all.

Aboveground disposal requires landowner permission and is not recommended for carcasses of sick (or suspected of being sick) animals. Choose isolated locations to reduce encounters with pets and people, and do not overuse a location. Sites should be 100 yards from surface water.

### Belowground, Individual Grave

Belowground disposal conceals the sights and smells of decomposition from people and scavengers. The digging of graves, however, can become quite laborious when used for several carcasses. All of the following conditions must be met for individual graves:

1. The carcass must be covered by at least 2 feet of soil within 24 hours after burial,
2. The carcass must not come into contact with surface or groundwater,
3. The grave must be located at least 200 feet from any groundwater well that is used to supply potable drinking water, and
4. The number of individual graves must not exceed 100 graves per acre.

### Belowground, Common Grave

All of the following conditions must be met for common graves:

1. Carcasses should be covered with at least 12 inches of soil within 24 hours after burial,
2. Carcasses must not come into contact with surface or groundwater and must not be disposed of in a 100 year floodplain or wetland area as defined by the Solid Waste Management Act,
3. The number of carcasses should not exceed 250,
4. Common graves should not remain open for more than 30 days,
5. They should have at least 4 feet of soil as final cover,
6. They must be located at least 200 feet from any groundwater well that is used to supply potable drinking water, and
7. The number of common graves should not exceed 5 graves per acre.

### Incineration

The incinerator must be approved by state and local authorities to burn animal carcasses. Incineration can cost more than $0.50 per pound, making it relatively expensive.

## Landfill

Carcasses taken to a landfill must be securely enclosed in a plastic bag or other suitable airtight container to prevent noxious odors. They may be disposed of at a Type-II, licensed, solid-waste disposal facility (standard landfill) or at an out-of-state facility in accordance with that state's solid waste disposal regulations.

## Resources

AVMA Guidelines on Euthanasia (2007) https://www.avma.org/KB/Policies/Documents/euthanasia.pdf (visited Oct. 26, 2012).

Chappell, M. S. 1999. A Model for Humane Reduction of Feral Cat Populations. http://www.stanford.edu/group/CATNET/articles/model_program.html (visited 2/9/2010); reprinted from *California Veterinarian* Sept/Oct, 1999.

Fitzwater, W. D. 1994. Feral Cats, in *Prevention and Control of Wildlife Damage*. Editors, Scott E. Hygnstrom, Robert M. Timm, Gary E. Larson. University of Nebraska–Lincoln. 2 vols.

Sharp, T. and G. Saunders. 2005. *CAT002 Trapping of feral cats use cage traps*. Natural Heritage Trust: NSW Department of Primary Industries. Australia. 10pp.

Vantassel, S. M., P. D. Curtis, and S. E. Hygnstrom. 2012. *National Wildlife Control Training Program: Core Principles*. University of Nebraska–Lincoln and Cornell University.

Chapter 10. **Closing Remarks**

I hope you found the book helpful in your efforts to control the impacts free-ranging cats have on our environment and your property. Be sure you follow the law, or as I have argued, be more than legal, be ethical. I welcome your comments, suggestions, photos, and even criticisms. Just send them to <u>wildlifecontrolconsultant@gmail.com</u>. All submissions become property of Wildlife Control Consultant, LLC and may be used to enhance future editions. Names are withheld unless you provide explicit permission to acknowledge your contribution by name.

You may be interested in my other publications available at Amazon.com and other fine retailers:

*Wildlife Damage Inspection Handbook*, 3rd ed. Lincoln, NE: Wildlife Control Consultant, LLC., 2012.

*Dominion over Wildlife: An Environmental-Theology of Human-Wildlife Relations.* Eugene, OR: Wipf & Stock, 2009).

# Other Books by Stephen M. Vantassel

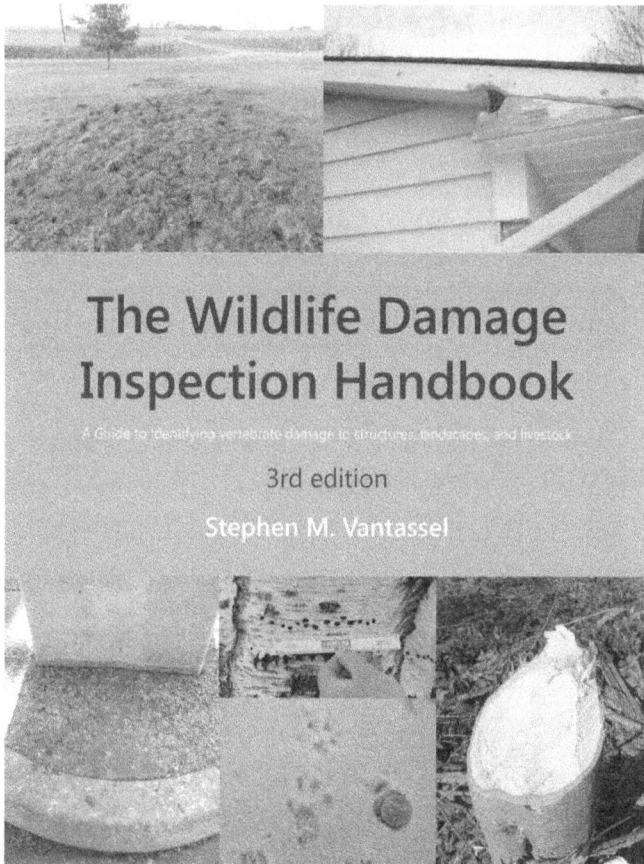

The Wildlife Damage Inspection Handbook

A Guide to identifying vertebrate damage to structures, landscapes, and livestock

3rd edition

Stephen M. Vantassel

*The Wildlife Damage Inspection Handbook* 3rd ed. is designed to help wild-life management professionals, pest management professionals, home inspectors, and property managers identify damage caused by vertebrate animals to structures, to landscapes, and to livestock.

The text has been revised thoroughly and expanded to provide more detailed information on more topics. The new layout and full color printing are accented by the large number of photos supporting the text.

The book is divided into two parts:

Part 1 explains the theory and practice of inspection and provides strategies to identify animals by feces, bones, and eye-shine.

Part 2 contains modules reviewing the damage left by the most common problem wildlife in the United States. Each species module summarizes the animal's biology, scat, diseases, and damage to property and livestock.

**Stephen M. Vantassel**

Foreward by **Tom C. Rakow**

# Dominion Over Wildlife?

An Environmental Theology
of Human-Wildlife Relations

In *Dominion over Wildlife: An Environmental-Theology of Human-Wildlife Relations*, Stephen M. Vantassel investigates the biblical, ethical, and scientific argument employed by the Christian Animal Rights movement concerning human-wildlife relations. Stephen addresses several important questions:

How should Christians treat our wildlife neighbors?

Has the Church been wrong in its understanding of human dominion?

Does God want Christians to avoid hunting, trapping, fishing, and adopt a vegetarian lifestyle?

Stephen provides answers to these questions using scripture, ethics, and science and concludes by detailing a perspective he calls, "Shepherdism."

Visit his website at http://wildlifecontrolconsultant.com.

www.ingramcontent.com/pod-product-compliance
Lightning Source LLC
Chambersburg PA
CBHW031446280326
41927CB00037B/375